EMPOWERING DISCIPLINE

THE APPROACH THAT *WORKS* WITH AT-RISK STUDENTS

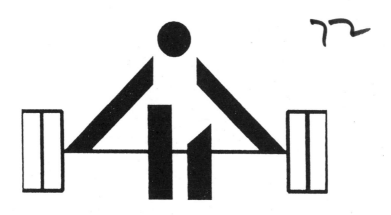

by
VICKI PHILLIPS

EMPOWERING DISCIPLINE

VICKI PHILLIPS

PERSONAL DEVELOPMENT PUBLICATIONS
P. O. Box 203
Carmel Valley, CA 93924

(831) 659-5913
(888) 4 AT-RISK
Fax: (831) 659-9109

EMPOWERING DISCIPLINE

INTRODUCTION

I am writing this book because I believe we have reached a stalemate in our attempts to deal with at-risk youth in mainstream schools. We fear that too many students are "out-of-control"; yet our attempts to regain control simply escalate the crisis. Everyone says that something *must be done,* yet nothing seems to work. As I see it, it is time to shift to a new paradigm. The "control paradigm" upon which most school discipline programs are based doesn't work with the very students we wish to change.

I was principal of an alternative high school for twenty-two years. All of our students were "at-risk." We developed a repetoire of very successful strategies which *did work.* But none of these strategies were based upon the "control paradigm." They were based upon what we know about what it takes to actually change human behavior and were more therapeutic than disciplinary in nature. AND THEY WORKED!

Several years ago I discovered the explanation of *why* these strategies worked better than the control paradigm. I learned that about 85% of my students came from a single personality temperament (David Keirsey's Personality Temperament Theory, from *PLEASE UNDERSTAND ME, 1978).* These students feel an intense need to be self-directed and resist being told what to do. I discovered that each of the four personality temperaments has its own teaching and learning style, and that the personality

1

temperament most typical of at-risk youth--the SP's--has the fewest teachers, only 7% of mainstream secondary teachers. Further, most of them teach Art, Music, P.E., Coaching, Vocational Education, or Alternative Education. Very few teach required mainstream classes. Yet SP's make up 40% of the population!

In the first Chapter we will look at the joys, strengths, and stressors of each of the four temperaments. You will discover that it is the SJ's that control mainstream education, along with the approach toward discipline used by all schools. You will learn that the joys and strengths of the SJ's are identical to the stressors of the SP's, and that what stresses the SJ's are identical to what brings joy to SP's! Since there are so few mainstream SP teachers, and since each temperament has its own teaching and learning style, SP's spend most of their school experience operating out of their areas of weakness and doing things which stress them. And then they are compared on a bell-shaped curve with students who are being taught in a way which emphasizes their strengths!

Are all of the students from this one temperament "at-risk"? Not at all. My theory is this: If a student is validated at home and then does not feel successful at school, he/she will probably be okay anyway. If a student is *not validated* at home, (perhaps the family is distracted by family problems, poverty, alcoholism, drugs, or a too-heavy work schedule), but he finds success in an extracurricular activity or at school, he will probably be okay as well. But if a student isn't validated anywhere--at home or through an extra-curricular outlet, *or* at school, she is much more likely to act out or to give up--making her likely to be at-risk. If you add to this the often twin factors of poverty and minority status, and if the student doesn't personally know any role models who have "made it" other than through gang activity, at-risk behavior is almost assured.

School works fine for most kids. But for those from this one temperament, the teachers' joys are the students' stressors. If you take the stress level these students experience at home and pile on the additional stress they experience at school, and if there is no positive validation to lessen the sense of hopelessness they feel, at-risk behavior is predictably the result. The population of my school represented only about 10% of the population of the two sending high schools, and as mentioned above, SP's represent about 40% of the population. But I believe that the many SP's who make it do so *in spite of* our educational system, not *because* of it.

Why is this important to us as we examine the predominating approach toward discipline in our schools (and in the Juvenile Justice System as well)? Because SP's don't respond well to being controlled; they react *worse,* not better. The fact that the majority of students *do* respond to a control model is irrelevant; these students are from a different personality temperament and "control" is not their push-button issue. But with the students whom we feel we most *need* to control, our methods do not work. We respond by calling them "bad kids." Actually, we are using "bad strategies." There are strategies which work really well with these students, but they do not grow out of the control model.

What do these "difficult students" want? They want to feel POWERFUL and IN CHARGE; they want to feel *SELF-DIRECTED.* We can work with this. I plan to show how we can *use* the need of these students to be "in control" so that they will no longer be "out of control." But this cannot happen until the current Control Paradigm which underlies traditional discipline is replaced by a new philosophy which attempts to "empower" students. We need to help them take control of their *own* behavior so they will stop putting all of their energy into resisting our attempts to control them. And although the "control" approach doesn't work with the students who don't want to be told what to do, Empowering Discipline, which I am advocating, works with *all* students.

3

PERSONALITY TEMPERAMENT AND LEARNING STYLES

David Keirsey's theory of Personality Temperament is based upon the work of Myers-Briggs, who developed the M.B.T.I. (Myers-Briggs Type Indicator) to measure personality type. The work of Isabelle Myers and her mother Katherine Briggs was, in turn, based upon the work of Carl Jung. Where Myers-Briggs identified sixteen personality types, David Keirsey simplified this work for practioners by identifying four temperaments, each of which contains four types. Each of Keirsey's temperaments has specific joys, strengths, stressors, and a teaching and learning style.

Turn to page 5 and spend a little time with it. Try to identify your own temperament. Then identify that most prevalent in mainstream education. Next find that of the typical at-risk student. Compare the Joys and Strengths of the SJ's with the Stressors and Frustrations of the SP's--and vice versa. You will see that SJ's value responsibility and "being prepared". They believe in work before pleasure. They *like* routine and structure and appreciate rules and direction. They *prefer* security, safety, and stability. They are *DIRECTED* learners; they need to be taught in a directed, sequential way in order to do their best work. SJ teachers tend to be stressed most by students who aren't "responsible", since responsibility is a major SJ value. In contrast, SP's need to feel *FREE* and want

NF's (Intuitive Feelers)

JOYS & STRENGTHS

Must live in INTEGRITY & be REAL
Seek the MEANING OF LIFE
Are PEOPLE-ORIENTED
Love to COMMUNICATE
Are GENTLE; Dislike conflict
Are EMPATHETIC; Value uniqueness
Are SINCERE and IDEALISTIC
Look for POTENTIAL in others

STRESSORS & FRUSTRATIONS

Being treated IMPERSONALLY
DISHARMONY & CONFLICT
Lack of communication, appreciation
Cool, reserved or insensitive people
Narrowminded, judgmental people
Rigidness and heartlessness
Details, procedures, red tape

NT's (Intuitive Thinkers)

JOYS & STRENGTHS

Are ANAYLTICAL & INTELLIGENT
Seek KNOWLEDGE, COMPETENCE
Relate on an INTELLECTUAL LEVEL
Prefer THINKING, LOGIC to feeling
Like to ARGUE and DEBATE
Want to know WHY; Seek ANSWERS
Are INDEPENDENT THINKERS
Value JUSTICE and FAIRNESS

STRESSORS & FRUSTRATIONS

Being treated as INCOMPETENT
Anything ILLOGICAL, disorganized
Emotional scenes or outbursts
People who don't value learning
Lack of freedom to pursue purpose
Making individual exception to the rule
Meetings with no purpose, distractions

SJ'S (Sensing Judgers)

JOYS & STRENGTHS

Are RESPONSIBLE, productive
Seek to BE PREPARED, PLAN
Seek work *before* pleasure
Value STABILITY, tradition
Like to FOLLOW RULES
ARE ORGANIZED, DECISIVE
Are loyal and dependable
Respect authority, chain of command

STRESSORS & FRUSTRATIONS

IRRESPONSIBILITY
People who don't follow the rules
Inefficiency and disorganization
Change or inconsistency
Having things feel "out of control"
Unreliable or disorganized people
People who don't take things seriously

SP'S (Sensing Perceivers)

JOYS & STRENGTHS

Need to feel FREE, SPONTANEOUS
Prefer UNSTRUCTURED settings
PLAYFUL. Work must be FUN!
Like to TAKE RISKS, try new things
Like to WORK AROUND RULES
Are RESOURCEFUL, FLEXIBLE
Are witty, clever, and CREATIVE
Are very egalitarian

STRESSORS & FRUSTRATIONS

Being told what they HAVE TO DO!
Feeling trapped or controlled
Boredom, sameness, predictability
Rigidness, inflexibility, rules
Having to plan first & follow a list
Timelines, schedules, paperwork
People who lack a sense of humor

© 1995 by Vicki Phillips

to keep their options open. This is because, at their best, they are highly resourceful and actually prefer the "adrenalin rush" which accompanies solving a crisis without preplanning. They are excellent troubleshooters and are very spontaneous, enjoying action, variety, and change. Unlike the SJ's, they prefer unstructured settings and need a lot of excitement and stimulation--and *FUN*--in order to learn. Highly creative and skillful, they need "hands-on" education in order to shine. They find it difficult to learn by reading *about* something--especially if they see no personal immediate need for the information. They learn best in a random, non-sequential way and when they are interested in the topic. What stresses them most is feeling controlled or trapped and being told what they *should* do.

According to Keirsey, 43% of high school teachers are SJ's, along with 45% of students.[1] Schools are run in a way which favors SJ's, and so SJ's of course are not at-risk. As I already mentioned, although 40% of students are SP's, only 7% of high school teachers are SP's (and they generally can be found in hands-on elective courses which aren't required for graduation). No wonder SP's are most likely to be at-risk. It is not an innate trait; it's in reaction to the way we have structured our schools. In the past they could always drop out and become apprentices in one of the trades or get a "hands-on" type of job and do fine. However, everyone needs *at least* a high school diploma to make it these days. Our drop-out rate has been dramatically reduced; yet we have not changed our schools to better meet the needs of the kinesthetic learner.

You might be thinking that all at-risk students are not alike. Remember, there are four personality types in each temperament. Some SP's are extraverts and some are introverts. Some are

---

[1] Statistics on students are from a speech by Dr. Keirsey at a Temperament Conference in Newport Beach, CA in June, 1996, correcting those given in his book *PLEASE UNDERSTAND ME* (1978). Statistics on teachers are from *EFFECTIVE TEACHING, EFFECTIVE LEARNING* by Alice and Lisa Fairhurst, 1995.

"feelers" and make decisions using their hearts not their heads, while others are "thinkers" and make unemotional, analytical decisions. As a result, there are wide variations in behavior within the SP temperament category. Also, each has a different environment to react to. All are alike, however, in their need for personal freedom and in their random, concrete approach to learning.

What about the other two temperaments? The NF's and the NT's are both abstract thinkers (where the SJ's and SP's are alike only in their both preferring concrete ideas). The NF's (Intuitive Feelers) represent just 9% of the students but a full 35% of high school teachers! NF's are people-oriented, love to communicate, tend to see the potential in others (and are therefore often thought of as "unrealistic" by those who are more "reality-based."). NF students tend to do well in school because they like learning and tend to want to please. Although NF's can be sensitive, there are almost four NF teachers to each NF student, looking to help with their problems! NF teachers often get frustrated with the SJ side of school, with its emphasis on planning, procedures, regulations, and red-tape. They want to put all their energy into working with youth.

The NT's (Intuitive Thinkers) represent just 6% of students and 15% of high school teachers. They love the pursuit of knowledge and the feeling of being competent. They are seen as very intelligent and analytical. They pride themselves on being logical and being able to put their feelings "on a shelf"; they don't like to get emotional, preferring thinking and logic over feeling. They are also very independent, wanting to learn their own way, by pursuing the answers to their "Why" questions.

Surprisingly, NT students can sometimes be "at-risk," primarily if they are taught in an unchallenging way or forced to do what they consider busywork. They see this as an insult to their intelligence and competence--and that is *their* push-button issue. Like the SP's, they don't like feeling "controlled", but since they love the pursuit of knowledge, they are much less at-risk than SP's. NT teachers tend to get frustrated with students who don't value learning, since that is their main value. And, like the NT students, they tend to get frustrated with the SJ side of school, with its meetings, policies, and procedures. Both NT teachers *and* students alike become frustrated with oversupervision.

Anyone who has been in education for awhile knows that the educational pendulum regularly swings back and forth, with different solutions to educational problems appearing, disappearing, and then later reappearing with different names attached. I believe that this phenomena is nothing more than the three main temperaments (the SJ's, the NT's, and the NF's) taking turns seizing control and insisting that their way is the *right* way for *all* students. (SP's are too few in number as teachers of mainstream classes to have ever "seized control" of the educational pendulum. But they can regularly be heard advocating for more electives and insisting upon the need for Vocational Education for the non-college bound.)

SJ's regularly push for the teaching of Basic Skills and see teaching as the imparting of separate discreet bits of information. They believe in Standardized Testing as a way to determine whether students are learning the information presented. SJ's advocate for the phonics method of teaching reading, the teaching of fact-based information in Social Studies, and for Back to the Basics in Math.

In contrast, NT's advocate for the Constructivist approach to learning and want students to be able to do more than "regurgitate facts"; they must be able to "make meaning." They stress the importance of teaching higher level thinking skills and critical thinking, and they prefer "authentic assessment", and "new math." NT's also regularly emphasize the importance of challenging the brightest students and the need to raise standards. Although only 15% of high school teachers are NT's (and far fewer elementary teachers), they tend to be visionary in their thinking and emphasize the need for strategic planning. Some find their way into key positions within the district in order to push for their ideas.

NF's, who like NT's are abstract thinkers, also want students to be able to "make meaning" rather than to memorize facts. But they also want the material to relate to the students' lives. They advocate for the "whole language" approach to the teaching of Language Arts rather than the phonics method. (NT's, as abstract thinkers, also prefer whole language to phonics but are more likely to be teaching Science or Math than Language Arts.) NF's also stress the need for "affective education" and the teaching of values and pro-social skills. And it is the NF's who urge a student-driven, success-oriented curriculum where the individual needs of students are emphasized more than standardized norms.

SJ's are not only in the majority when it comes to teaching positions, they are in an even *greater* majority when it comes to administration. More than any other temperament, they love to organize, and they aspire to positions where they can organize even larger groups of people, such as a school rather than just a classroom, or the district rather than just a school. Also, they enjoy committee work, which isn't as naturally appealing to the other temperaments. As a result, they usually form the majority bloc which controls most committees and they thus dominate to an even greater extent than their numbers would indicate.

Traditional discipline tends to reflect the assumptions of the educational system's SJ majority: that the teacher should be "in charge" and the students' role is to follow directions and to be responsible. These beliefs are supported by the Anglo-Germanic cultural heritage of this country. The Puritain work ethic and the Germanic emphasis on following orders have entertwined in a way that gives great credibility and almost unquestioned support of the concepts underlying traditional school discipline. Besides, it is mainly the SJ majority which is most concerned that students do what they are told. NF's are more concerned with changing the students' behavior in connection with developing their potential, and they often express concern about the control paradigm being too rigid and try to "humanize" it and look for exceptions for certain students. But the establishment of rules and control is not one of their major interests. Nor is it to the NT's or the few SP's, as both temperaments tend to dislike being controlled personally and are less likely to be interested in creating a system by which to control others; thus, SJ's are left "in control" of the area of control.

Alfie Kohn decried the reliance on controlling students in his thought-provoking book *BEYOND DISCIPLINE* (ASCD, 1996). But his solutions seem better geared for NT's and NF's, the abstract thinkers, than for SP's, who don't necessarily share the appreciation of "higher level thinking skills" and the "making of meaning" in class and who need to be *DOING* something fun, relevant to *their* needs, and involving a concrete payoff. For SP's, learning is not necessarily its own reward.

Because the majority of teachers are SJ's, schools tend to favor the SJ students, who want to be directed, responsible, and *will* follow the rules. NF students generally don't like conflict and want to please, so they tend to go along with the program as well. NT students love to learn, so although they have an independent streak, school *is* about learning, and with the right teachers, they excel! Then there are the SP's--who *don't* like to be told what to do, and who certainly *don't* do their best when taught the way most mainstream teachers teach. So which of the four temperaments is most likely to regularly confront the "control paradigm" on a regular basis? The very students who face the most frustration in our schools, the way we have structured them, and who are least likely to submit to our attempts at being "in control"! Hence, the problem!

BEHAVIORIST THEORY
Versus
AT-RISK STUDENTS

Traditional Discipline is based upon Behaviorist theory. The concept is that if you reward good behavior and punish bad behavior, students will adopt good behavior and eliminate bad behavior in an attempt to gain the rewards and avoid the punishments. However, the experimentation which supports Behaviorist Theory was done in laboratories with mice. Mice could be trained to push the lever which would give them food and to ignore the lever which would shock them. My question is this: "Do mice care what other mice think?" And do they have a basic need, as adolescent SP's seem to have, to appear "clever, impressive, and free" before their peers? (Delunas, 1992).

Also, how *big* are the rewards that schools are able to offer? Can schools afford to offer a payoff big enough so that an SP adolescent is willing, in his own mind, to "humiliate" himself in front of his peers by complying? Besides, since most schools use a bell-shaped curve and the student finds herself competing with students who *are* being taught in their learning style (which (s)he is not), is it likely that the student feels she'll be one of the winners? And if he has always been told that "the way you're going, you'll never amount to anything anyway" and if he believes it, will he feel that it makes sense to make any sacrifices for the future?

And what about the punishments available? You can give students detention or suspend them. What happens if you give them detention and they skip it? You can give them double detention. If they skip that you can give them quadruple detention. Pretty soon they are seventeen years old with seven years of detention and you know you have no control. Or you can suspend them--for up to five days at a time. Do they care? Not if they don't have any aspirations anyway. They just reframe the situation and call it a five-day *vacation*. And then they come back--often with an attitude. THEY HAVE TENURE!

Many of these students cannot visualize themselves as adults. They say things like "I'll never live past twenty-one anyway." So they really have nothing to lose by acting up. At least they can feel "clever, impressive, and free" as they tell you off and strut out of the room after you have announced their negative consequence of suspension. They feel like they have won! No wonder they don't change.

Besides, disruptive adolescents can sense that they usually have the support of their peers. Adolescence is the period where it is almost the student's "job description" to revolt against adult authority. Teenagers are trying to achieve their independence from "those in charge" in preparation for the time, not too far off, when they too will become adults. Even generally compliant students seem to secretly envy the rebels, almost as if they were thinking "I wish I had that kind of nerve!" Look at the "role models" teenagers extol-- both on television and through their music. The theme is rebellion and power--certainly not compliance with adult authority.

Traditional discipline plans disempower kids; the emphasis is on what they *can't* do. They start by clearly listing all rules and the exact consequences which will occur with each infraction. This approach can become a *challenge* to SP students. When you tell them what *not* to do, you often make the behavior *more,* not less, desirable. And they pride themselves on their ability to circumvent obstacles--including rules and regulations. The more you try to "control" them, the more you are seen as limiting their autonomy, the more they will try to outsmart you--and the more they will lock themselves into a downhill spiral of self-defeating behavior.

Lately there has been much advocacy of the Zero Tolerance concept. Educators pride themselves on how little negative behavior they will tolerate! Journalists have had a field day writing up seemingly ridiculous situations whereby honor students are expelled for having a Midol in a purse or a fish filleting knife (along with other fishing gear) in a backpack. Meanwhile student drug use and gang behavior show few signs of disappearing. Schools *have* managed to remove problem students. But they have not managed to help them change their behavior. Their negative behaviors are often turned loose upon their communities without appropriate intervention. And as the wave of school shootings have proved, especially the one in Oregon which occured the day after a suspension, students can say "NO!" to Zero Tolerance by returning to school armed. *"Don't tell me where I can't go!"* can be the response. Students aren't necessarily safe from a disaffected student, even when he is banned from campus.

On a less dramatic note, teachers everywhere complain about the lack of motivation in many youth today. I believe that you can't build motivation in at-risk students in an environment where they feel powerless, because the need to gain the feeling of power will dominate their energy. Motivation does not grow out of the obedience model. No one can "get excited" about doing someone else's thing!

Obviously, we need a different approach--one which doesn't negatively escalate behavior and destroy motivation. A more therapeutic model is needed to replace the control model--one which really *changes* negative behavior and builds hope. But it must be one which can easily be used by existing teaching staff. The strategies need to be understandable and workable. And they need to work with the very students who have problems in our schools--the students who "don't want to be told what to do".

I believe that EMPOWERING DISCIPLINE is such a model. I have developed it as I worked with the at-risk students who comprised the entire population of the school where I was principal for over two decades. It was highly influenced by my counseling background and shaped by my personal experiences (both successes and failures) as I tried to change the negative student behavior patterns I kept seeing in my students. It also reflects a variety of influences to whom I give credit in the Bibliography.

I have been giving teacher workshops for almost three years now, and many teachers have contacted me afterwards to let me know that these methods work so much better for them than the traditional approach to discipline. Several teachers even said that they had been on the verge of giving up teaching because of the power struggles that seemed to result each time they tried to get their at-risk students "under control". They each said that the entire picture had changed. They no longer had an adversarial relationship with their students and teaching had actually become enjoyable!

In workshops I have developed four sequential steps to implementing this new approach to discipline. I call the steps the **FOUR D's of DISCIPLINE:**

(1) **D**evelop supportive relationships;

(2) **D**evelop a classroom which is Structured for Success;

(3) **D**efuse (**D**etach, **D**isengage, and **D**e-escalate) potential problems at the lowest possible level;

(4) **D**ebrief later so students can learn from mistakes.

I will share these steps and the strategies which supports them. I will also share the underlying assumptions for both the Traditional and the Empowering Discipline approaches. Then *you* can choose.

Note that the first two "D's" are preventative in nature. Empowering Discipline is a *pro*-active approach, in contrast to Traditional Discipline, which I see as reactive in nature. Some discipline programs *say* they believe in prevention, and some do talk about the need to treat students respectfully. However, I don't see them advocating changing anything about the teaching style used in order to better meet these students' needs and prevent their frustration. Likewise, I don't see them suggesting that students be *empowered*, so that they can "take charge" of their lives and become aware of the choices they do have. Nowhere is it suggested that students need to feel *more*, rather than less, powerful before they can become *self*-disciplined. These, I believe, are critical pieces which must be addressed.

Empowering Discipline seeks to set the stage for student success *ahead of time* by providing what they *need*. At-Risk students won't change their attitude toward school if they feel unwelcome, incompetent, and *over-controlled* there. I once heard an analogy that fits well here: If you are downstream and find yourself having to continue to rescue student after student, all of whom are struggling to keep from drowning as the river current sweeps them by, wouldn't it make sense to send someone upstream to find out why so many are falling into the river in the first place? Then you could *prevent* the many near-drownings. The first two D's of the Empowering Discipline plan attempt to keep students from becoming discipline problems in the first place.

DEVELOPING
SUPPORTIVE RELATIONSHIPS

One of the main things which at-risk youth need from you is your support. They may not always look like they are looking for your support. Many have hardened. They expect adults to look down on them; this is how it's always been for them and why should you be any different? Many will reject new adults in their lives *first*, before the new adults can reject them. Yet, developing a positive and supportive relationship with your at-risk students is the foundation for everything else you do. Without this foundation, none of the other strategies will prove enough to make the difference for these students.

In order to change these negative attitudes, we have to make sure that our own attitude is positive. IT TAKES A *POSITIVE* ATTITUDE TO CHANGE A *NEGATIVE* ATTITUDE! Ask any Math teacher: If you wish to change a negative to a positive, what do you need to add? A POSITIVE which is *larger* than the negative. If you add·a negative to a negative, you simply get a larger negative!

Teachers are often concerned about not having the time it takes to build a positive relationship with each student. My answer is always that it doesn't *have* to take a lot of time. At-risk youth are wary at first of adults who attempt to overwhelm them with their presence and their desire to relate to students. They don't want a casework relationship with you. They prefer a more casual, less time-intensive involvement.

Therefore, I have taken the term "Carpe Diem!" from the movie "The Dead Poet's Society" and changed it to the more realistic "Carpe Momento!" Make sure you constantly project an open, encouraging, "invitational" persona so that students will see you as someone they could turn to if they did have a problem. Greet students at the door. Treat them as individuals. Get to know them better by including Journal Writing as a regular beginning of each class period. Remember, if they like you they will more likely want to please you, which in turn will make your job a lot easier. You are not trying to win a popularity contest; however, if you like them, they will like you. Then you will have more influence with them.

The first need that at-risk students have is no different than the first need all students have--to have someone *believe* in them. Someone else must believe in them before they can believe in themselves. The Resiliency Research has made it clear that being respected by a caring, responsible adult is a key to turning an at-risk outlook into a resilient one. Lucky young people have had one or more of these caring adults since birth--and call them mom or dad, or better yet, mom *and* dad. These children did not have to prove their worthiness *before* they were loved; their parents knew they were special from Day One. Other children found this support from a grandparent, or an aunt, or a pre-school teacher, or a grade school teacher. The unlucky children are still looking for this support.

What about the students who are hard to like? Every honest teacher has had students like that. It helps to remember that you would probably understand even your worst student's behavior better if you knew his or her story. Many at-risk students have been abused--physically, emotionally, often even sexually--which has resulted in their distrusting adults. Many are faced daily with overwhelming stress and yet most lack in their lives positive adult role models to show them how to deal with it. So they either withdraw or act out aggressively. Think about this: When students are stressed, you have a choice. You can either help them set down the stress or pile more on. If they are "on the edge", you can either pull them back or push them over!

Students will not act in positive ways until they start *seeing* themselves in positive ways. We all act according to the way we *SEE* ourselves. And yet in education, we've been trained to look for *negatives!* We constantly label students--and few of these labels are positive. We diagnose and we remediate. We look for limitations so we can "fix" them. The problems start when students *believe* us! What does a "disobedient" student do? Disobey! Instead we should be looking for strengths or potential strengths to help students develop. Students need to be defined by what they are *good* at; they will not change their behavior for the better by having us define them in terms of what they are *not* good at! Labels can build people up or tear them down.

Each of the four personality temperaments focuses on different sets of values around which to develop behavior. SP's value spontaneity, freedom, fun, creativity, and resourcefulness, and when they aren't given a positive outlet for their expression, they will often find a negative outlet. SJ's, in contrast, value responsibility, stability, planning, work before pleasure, and they often look at SP behavior as "irresponsible" when it conflicts with their own needs. Understanding Temperament theory can help us be less judgmental by allowing us to look at student behavior from a different perspective.

Review the LIABILITIES TO ASSETS list, page 19. Most of the pairs of words can be looked at in either way. Often a liabiity is simply too much of a potentially good thing. Someone who expresses too much leadership potential--all the time!--is seen as bossy! Challenge yourself to always look for the potential assets in your students. This list below will help. Simply look for the negative behavior which bothers you and then "translate" it into a potential asset. Students will be much more receptive to you if you talk to them about the potential asset you see in them--such as determination or tenacity--and ask if they would be interested in learning how to express it so that they wouldn't keep getting suspended! Students, like everyone else, can't resist being admired. Be a Talent Scout. Look for things to admire about your students.

LIABILITIES TO ASSETS

Short attn span	Many interests
Irresponsible	Carefree
Distractible	Perceptive
Hyperactive	Energetic
Unpredictable	Flexible
Impulsive	Spontaneous
Loud	Enthusiastic
Stubborn	Persistent
Poor Planner	Present-Oriented
Disorganized	Unstructured
Willful	Determined
Bossy	Leadership
Argumentative	Committed
Tests limits	Risk-Taker
Manipulative	Negotiator
Anxious	Cautious
Impatient	Eager
Explosive	Dramatic
Disobedient	Self-Directed
Rebellious	Non-conformist
Defiant	Bold

Sometimes you might have to stretch the truth a bit in identifying an "asset", but this is just your *starting* point! They can "grow into it"!

You will have much more influence with your students if you use OPTIMISM as a strategy and see them "AS IF not AS IS." Besides, it will shift your own attitude and your approach in working with the students. Seeing a student as self-directed, for example, will call for far different behavior from you than seeing the same student as disobedient! Remember that you will never be able to get a student to change WHO he or she is. But you can help that student become a HEALTHY and POSITIVE version of who he or she is rather than an unhealthy and negative version. (For example, you can help a *rude* and *defiant* student become *bold* and *direct*-- but *not* shy and submissive.) I believe the following:

Students
will change only if
we honor *who they are now*
and help them discover how
they might become more
of *who they are now*
by making some
CHANGES.

© 1996 by Vicki Phillips

Understanding Temperament Theory helps us understand who our students are trying to be. We can help them make it *positive!*

Part of developing a supportive environment involves teaching students to support each other. You are not the only person in your room whose attitude needs to be positive. It is very fashionable for adolescents to "cap on" each other--to put each other down. Talk to them about how harmful this is. Tell them that the research shows that it takes five positive strokes to counteract each putdown--just to get the student back to neutral! Explain this to your students. Talk about how when they go to a football or a basketball game they cheer for their team, since that helps them play better. They don't jeer them. Tell them that you want a supportive atmosphere in your classroom.

I highly recommend the book *THE NIBBLE THEORY* by Kaleel Jamison (1989). The book, which contains many illustrations, shows each individual as a circle. Jamison says that personal growth is all about making your own circle bigger. Sometimes people who are small circles feel uncomfortable around those who are BIG circles so they try to "take a bite out of them" to help equalize their sizes. Jamison explains that the way to get bigger is not to nibble in order to make others smaller. He further explains that *everybody* can be bigger, without anyone having to be smaller! It's a fun book which can lead to great discussions and even writing assignments. One teacher I know got her class to decide that if anyone put anyone else down, that person owed the person who was put down five "put-ups" or strokes, to even things out!

At-risk students generally do not respond well to rules. They feel that rules are meant to be broken! But I have found that they do respond well to short discussions about values, expecially if you start by asking them how *they* want to be treated. They will respond with all the things that you want to tell *them* about how to treat *others!* Help them, through brainstorming, develop a CLASS-ROOM CODE OF ETHICS, which represents an agreement about how they will treat each other. One teacher, after a thorough discussion, saw her class reduce the brainstormed list to three critical words: RESPECT, BELONG, WORK. Another class came up with four "agreements":

        (1) Respect others;

        (2) Appreciate diversity;

        (3) Conduct yourself with honor;

        (4) Do your best work.

You can bet that both teachers played an active role in that discussion--asking the right questions and summarizing at the right places. But this sort of discussion is so much more effective with at-risk youth than making a list of what they *can't* do. Instead, establishing a sense of "This is how we do things in this room" will result in higher expectations, far more positive behavior, and better attitudes than any other method. Meanwhile, classroom problem-solving becomes a logical outgrowth of having the class develop a Code of Conduct. Students become part of the solution instead of the "problem" which the teacher is trying to keep "under control."

TEACHING
PRO-SOCIAL SKILLS

If you wish to change the behavior of your At-Risk students, you need to do more than clearly explain the rules and procedures to be followed. Rather than worry about how to *control anti*-social behavior, you will find that it is more effective to teach them *pro*-social skills and attitudes. But there is a definite way that it needs to be done if it is to "take", which is what we will cover in this Chapter. You will need to have first established a positive and supportive relationship with your students so that you will have the influence you need to teach them new values and skills. Without this relationship, they will reject any attempt to shape their outlook.

With a supportive relationship, students will start responding in a much more positive way to you. You might think that they have changed. Maybe you will think that the relationship is enough, and that perhaps they don't *need* to be taught a different attitude. However when you are not around, and when others treat them in a less supportive way, they often revert to their previous behavior.

We learned this the hard way at my school. We worked really hard on relationships, and students spoke of it feeling like "family" on campus. Student behavior became very positive. We tried not to look at the fact that when even our best students elected to return to the comprehensive high school, they generally were not successful and would be sent back to us, with stories to tell about how poorly they had been treated. We suspected that their behavior might have helped contribute to the reactions they had received.

We slowly realized that real change must mean that our students should eventually be able to succeed in *any* environment. As a staff, we decided to take a first step toward this goal by developing a one-week course for all new students focusing on those attitudes and values it would take for students to be successful in the *real* world. We knew that they would not always be in the sheltered environment we had provided. We spent considerable time as a staff brainstorming what should be taught, and chose five topics--Self-Esteem, Communication Skills, Goal-Setting, Decision-Making, and Responsibility.

At the time I was not familiar with the concept of Personality Temperament, but I was aware that we would have to package our message in terms that would appeal to students who value power over responsibility and who resist being told what to do. Since I was the one with the counseling background (and also was the principal!), I guided the course development, making certain that the five three hour sessions, each developed by a different team of teachers, each fit the overall theme of becoming "empowered". We had the students evaluate the course upon completing it, and when we received mainly A's, I decided that we were onto something!

Then students started asking for an Advanced Guidance course. We had given them fifteen hours of Guidance upon entry, and then that was the end of it; they were scheduled into English, Social Studies, Science, Math, and Art, with no further mention of the Guidance content. I looked around for a program to purchase and couldn't find any that I felt would appeal to our students. Since it was almost summer and since I had just purchased a new computer, I decided that I would do it myself--thinking it would take me a couple of months, and certainly not realizing that it would take over my life and become my driving passion!

One excellent advantage to working with at-risk students is that they give you lots of feedback. When I piloted the expanded one-semester course, which I called *PERSONAL DEVELOPMENT*, I realized that I was basically on-target with over 90% of the material. But anytime my students were bored for over a minute and a half, they would give me the "gift" of letting me know! So I was able to go back and "fix" parts that didn't quite work. I continued to co-teach the course with all of my staff members over the next five years, until it really worked flawlessly, no matter who was teaching.

A year after I began to market it I discovered an excellent paper written in 1991 by Bonnie 'Benard from Northwest Regional Educational Lab in Portland, Oregon. Her topic was the Protective Factors which build Resiliency. She had reviewed everything in the research on why some students, who really should be at-risk due to the at-risk factors in their lives, are not. Why had they been able to make it? She came up with a number of common themes which she called the "protective factors." I was delighted, because I had built all of these protective factors into my curriculum! As a practioner, I hadn't consulted the research; I had simply consulted my own experience and what I knew my students needed, and I attempted to present it in a way they would accept. Now, thanks to Bonnie Benard, I had a research base! I stopped talking about changing dysfunctional attitudes and started talking about building resiliency by teaching certain skills and attitudes directly and by providing the type of environment in which it flourishes.

What were the protective factors? I mentioned the first one earlier under Supportive Relationships--the need to have someone else believe in them unconditionally. (This factor of course cannot be provided by a curriculum; but it *can* be provided by you!) This relationship leads to the ability to form positive relationships with others. The other protective factors include the following:

- The ability to see oneself as *IN CHARGE OF* one's destiny;
- A sense of *PURPOSE;*
- *GOAL*-directedness;
- A *SUCCESS* orientation;
- a *BELIEF in a BRIGHT FUTURE*;
- the sense that the environment is *predictable* and has *meaning;*
- *PROBLEM-SOLVING SKILLS.*

Research found that resilient students shared certain traits:

- They had a *positive attitude* that brought out a similar positive response and helpfulness in others;

- They had *goals* for the future and a *sense of hope,* in spite of any negative circumstances in their lives. They honestly believed they could achieve their long-term goals, and they made good choices *in spite of* any problems;

- They seemed to feel they were *in charge of* their lives. When they were asked what they felt contributed to their success or failure in a situation, they pointed to what *they* had done or not done. They seemed to have an internal locus of control. They didn't *blame* others or play victim.

I have discovered that these concepts can be *taught* to at-risk students and that they will be enthusiastic about them. But two conditions are necessary. First, these concepts must be taught by someone the students respect. Second, the course must be presented as an opportunity for students to learn how to be successful even in environments that they feel are dysfunctional for them. If, instead, these concepts are perceived by the students as an attempt by the school to "straighten them out", they will resist. Not only do these youth not want to told *what to do*: they also do not want to be told *what to think!*

PERSONAL DEVELOPMENT is an eighty lesson, one semester course designed primarily for students (or young adults) thirteen years or older. It is available in either a Group or an Individualized version, and in a combined set. The Group version contains everything a teacher needs to present a group class. The Individualized version is suitable for Independent Study or for make-up lessons for students who have missed group classes. I call the main concepts of the curriculum Resiliency Skills.

RESILIENCY SKILLS

(1) Being able to recognize your own strengths and abilities, even in the absence of positive outside reinforcement;

(2) Understanding that your happiness is not dependent upon what happens TO you--that you CHOOSE whether to be happy or unhappy, positive or negative, powerful or a victim, by choosing what to focus on;

(3) Relating in a respectul and assertive way, knowing that "You get what you give";

(4) Understanding that taking responsibility means being POWERFUL and in charge of your own life, while not being responsible means playing victim, making excuses, blaming others, and waiting for others to take the initiative;

(5) Being able to CHOOSE your own abilities or behaviors, regardless of the situation or the provocation;

(6) Developing the confidence that you can make things happen;

(7) Using positive self-talk to motivate yourself to succeed;

(8) Choosing to take positive risks and to learn from any mistakes, instead of being discouraged by them;

(9) Understanding that you can shape your life the way you want through goal-setting and conscious decision-making;

(10) Using the power of visualization to make dreams happen.

© 1992 by Vicki Phillips

As I mentioned earlier, the ability to discover one's strengths, the first Resiliency Skill, cannot be directly taught. It depends upon someone else--a responsible adult--seeing positive assets in a young person that he or she isn't aware of, and *believing* in him or her. That is why it is so important that we look for strengths and assets, not deficits, in students. Ultimately students can be taught to look for and to reinforce themselves for their strengths, but someone else must do this for them first.

The second resiliency skill involves the recognition that we are each responsible for our own happiness--that we *choose* to be happy or unhappy, positive or negative, powerful or a victim--that it all depends on what we *FOCUS* on. Most of our students are very wrapped up in the problems confronting them daily. When good things do happen, they are happy, but more often, bad things happen and they feel sad or angry. They don't see that they have any choice in their attitude. We must convince them that they *do* have a choice; otherwise, how can they be *POWERFUL?* Their attitude would be outside of their control, leaving them at the mercy of others.

The Colors Exercise can teach students that they *do* have control of their attitude. Ask the students to look around the room and memorize everything that is a certain dominant color. (Avoid colors that are gang-related!) Give them thirty seconds and then have them close their eyes. Ask them to call out everything they remember that is _____ (Name a *different* dominant color.) They will find it hard to remember very many items and will complain that you cheated!

Explain that there is a part of the brain called the Reticular Activating System. Its job is that of a Gatekeeper. Since there are constantly so *many* sensory perceptions, their Gatekeepers' job is to keep out any perceptions that are not *directly* related to their goals or what they are looking for. If they try to remember all the *green* things, the Gatekeeper will let in perceptions of all the green things but try to block all other colors. If you ask them for the purple things, they might remember one or two which managed to slip by the Gatekeeper, but for the most part, they will draw a blank.

You can explain that some people are always looking for the

things which *aren't* right; others are always looking for things which make them laugh. Ask: Who will be happier? This can lead to great discussions about optimism versus pessimism and what it takes to be happy. The goal here is to help students understand that being happy and positive is a CHOICE. You can ask your students how can they be *POWERFUL* if their happiness is dependent only on what happens *to* them.

There are a number of programs available which teach social skills. Students can be taught skills such as those needed for conflict resolution. But my experience is that students will not elect to use the skills taught in *real* situations unless their attitudes have changed as well. We all want our students to be RESPONSIBLE. Yet we realize that our at-risk students do *not* go to bed at night dreaming about how they can be more responsibile the next day!

In changing student attitudes, we have to consider their personality temperament and *its* values. SP's value personal freedom and keeping their options open. They see "being good" and "being responsible" as doing what *someone else* wants them to do. It is only when you reframe the behavior you want from them as being *POWERFUL* behavior that they will aspire to it, because it will then match their core values.

How can you do this? I have found that if you are initially too direct and obvious in your teaching of values, at-risk youth will discover ways to play devil's advocate in order to keep from being told "what to think"! I discovered that new concepts can best be introduced indirectly, through poetry, metaphors, or analogies which students are challenged to "figure out." Then, after they have solved the "puzzle", you can apply *their answer* to a real, concrete situation. I found the perfect poem to teach the concept of responsibility in the poem "AUTOBIOGRAPHY IN FIVE SHORT CHAPTERS."

What I had hoped to change with a lesson around this poem was the tendency of my students to make excuses and blame others whenever anything went wrong. Their motive for this was, of course, to "get off the hook." If it was someone else's fault, they wouldn't have to receive any consequences, and they wouldn't have to change. They could keep doing what they were doing. What I wanted them to see was that whenever they blamed anyone else, they were "giving away their power." If that situation ever came up again, there would be nothing they could do about it. They had chosen to become a victim--someone without power.

You can start by explaining to your students that this is a *symbolic* autobiography, and so the author, who is unknown, didn't *really* "fall in a hole." But he or she kept doing something that was "dysfunctional" and caused problems. Explain that there is a VICTIM part of the poem and a POWERFUL part. Their job is to figure out which part of the poem is the victim part and which part is the powerful part--and also which is the ultimate VICTIM line and which is the ultimate POWER line Read the poem to them with feeling. They will all "get" that "It's not my fault!" is the ultimate victim line and that "It is my fault!" is the ultimate power line. Then *you* can play devil's advocate by asking how could it be his (or her) fault, since (s)he didn't dig the hole! They will quickly explain that the author was dumb enough to keep walking straight ahead at first and falling in, instead of looking for another way to go.

You can then ask how many of them like the word "fault", explaining that you personally don't like the word, since it is such a *blaming* word. They will agree that they don't like the word. Then you can help them brainstorm substitutions for the word, helping them come up with "looking for your personal power in a situation" or "assuming responsibility for what you can *do* to make things turn out well." You can get them to agree that it is smarter to look for

AUTOBIOGRAPHY IN FIVE SHORT CHAPTERS

(1) I walk, down the street.
   There is a deep hole in the sidewalk.
   I fall in.
   I am lost....I am hopeless.
      IT ISN'T MY FAULT.
   It takes forever to find a way out.

(2) I walk down the same street.
   There is a deep hole in the sidewalk.
   I pretend I don't see it.
   I fall in again.
   I can't believe I am in the same place.
      BUT IT ISN'T MY FAULT.
      It still takes a long time to get out.

(3) I walk down the street.
   There is a deep hole in the sidewalk.
   I see it is there.
   I still fall in....It's a habit.
      My eyes are open.
   I know where I am.
      IT IS MY FAULT.
   I get out immediately.

(4) I walk down the same street,.
   There is a deep hole in the sidewalk.
   I walk around it.

(5) I walk down another street.

                                    Author Unknown

31

what *you can do* in a situation instead of looking for what you *can't control*.

Next, review several real life case studies for them to discuss and role play. One can be that a teacher accuses them of cheating on a test. They *didn't* cheat. What are all their options? List their suggestions on the board without comment, (even if their suggestions include cursing the teacher out!). Then return to each item on the list, asking what would probably happen if they chose that particular option. This exercise will show that they can dramatically affect the outcome of a situation, even one which "wasn't their fault", *if* they react POWERFULLY by thinking of the possible consequences *ahead* of time, looking for what *they* can do to secure a positive outcome, instead of blaming someone else.

At-risk students must be further shown that, to be powerful, they must be free to CHOOSE their OWN attitudes and behaviors and not let other people "push their buttons." Ask your students: "If someone tries to 'push your buttons' and you give them the response they want by reacting angrily, who is 'in charge'?" and "Do POWERFUL people let other people push their buttons?" It is very *powerful* to remain in control of yourself and not let somone else hook you into reacting, which is being in the "VICTIM mode."

At-Risk students love the concept of POWER. Unfortunately, they often interpret this as power *over others* rather than power over themselves. This is an attitude that we must try to change. At-Risk students must be helped to understand that Being Powerful means being able to CONTROL ONESELF--not others. You can pick a student to ask: "If I wanted to CONTROL you and you didn't want to be controlled, could I do it?" He will inevitably answer that you couldn't. You can then respond that this is how *everyone* is. Some might *seem* to comply, but the minute you're not looking, they'll go back to doing what they want. Explain, however, that there is a very clever way to get others to change their behavior--and that is by changing what *you* do. If you change what you do, it will no longer be appropriate for others to react the way they had planned. They will have to change. Explain that this is what real control and power are--control over YOURSELF, so that no one else can push your buttons, and so you can act in ways that will bring you the best outcome.

It is important for At-Risk students to learn how they CAN control their feelings so that others can no longer "make them mad." The most helpful theory is Albert Ellis' Rational-Emotive Therapy, which he shared in *A NEW GUIDE TO RATIONAL LIVING,* 1975. Ellis explains that after something happens, and before your feelings "hook in", you interpret the event and "tell yourself" something about it. If you "awfulize" or "catastrophize" the event and tell yourself that you "CAN'T STAND IT!", your feelings will be much more extreme and harder to keep under control than if you tell yourself that the event was unfortunate but that you *know* you can handle it. The trick is to take CONTROL OF YOUR SELF-TALK! Instead of telling yourself that something it *terrible* and that you *can't stand it,* tell yourself that you *CAN* HANDLE IT and ask yourself what you can DO to make things better.

Students can be taught that one way they can live POWER-FULLY is to take responsibility for their own self-talk (their thinking). *PERSONAL DEVELOPMENT* incorporates Maxwell Maltz's theory of Psycho-Cybernetics (1960) which teaches that self-talk represents directions to the brain as to how to interpret events, how to feel, what actions to take, and even what is possible for us in life. Our brains are actually computers, and like computers, if we fill our brains with wrong information, our brains will accept the input as true and base decisions upon it. (Garbage in; garbage out!) So, as Henry Ford said, "If you think you CAN or you CAN'T, you are correct!"

This last concept can to used to counteract the "glass ceilings" that the majority of At-Risk students use to limit their potential. Most cannot visualize a positive future for themselves, which all too often becomes a self-fulfilling prophecy. You can teach them where their self-image comes from. It is result of the programming of our "computer-brain" before we are five years old--and most of the programming comes from other people. At-risk youth generally come from at-risk homes, and the "programming" is often negative, such as "You'll never amount to anything!" or "Can't you do *anything* right?" or "I wish I had never had you. You have certainly messed up my life!" Since most at-risk adolescents don't want anyone else to tell them what to do, they certainly don't want to accept negative programming from anyone else! In fact, this brain-as-computer analogy can be effectively used whenever a student says that he doesn't want to change because then "I wouldn't be ME!" You can simply gently ask who *is* he, really--the person who was programmed by *someone else* before he was five years old, or the person whom he *chooses* to be now that he is seventeen (or whatever his age). This approach always seems to defuse any reluctance to change.

You can teach your students that positive self-talk will make them stronger, and then you can prove it with the Arm Exercise. Ask for a volunteer. Have the volunteer hold his/her arm straight out to the side at shoulder level. Tell her you want to test her strength and that you will try to push her arm down. (Push down at the wrist.) Then explain that you will ask her to say different things which she is to say *with conviction* while you continue to test for strength by pushing down on her wrist. Have her first say, "My right (or left if she is left-handed) arm is *so weak!*" Her arm will

34

seem to lose power. Then have her say, "My right arm is *SO STRONG!*" Her arm will seem to gain strength. Then have her think of a time when she did something stupid and not to share it but to say something like "I can't believe I did anything *that stupid!* I'm *so embarrassed...*" Again, her arm will get weak. Then ask her to think of something outstanding which she has done and to tell everyone how *AWESOME* she was and to really get into feeling PROUD! Again her arm will become strong. Have everyone try it. Explain that their self-talk can strengthen or weaken them, and so to be very careful what they tell themselves!

At-Risk students often hesitate to try something new because they expect to do poorly and would rather say they aren't interested. Talk to them about taking positive risks and how necessary this is if they are to grow. Have everyone draw a circle. Explain that this represents their Comfort Zone. When they were born it was very small because everything they did was new and therefore somewhat scary. Tell them that the only way they can become more powerful is to s-t-r-e-t-c-h their Comfort Zone, even though this will feel uncomfortable at the time. The bigger their Comfort Zone the more POWERFUL they will be. Have them write inside their Comfort Zone circle all the things that *used* to scare them that no longer do. Then have them write outside their Comfort Zone circle all the things that still seem frightening which they would like to set as goals to achieve. Explain that successful people have as many fears as anyone else, but they just acknowledge these fears and act in spite of them. As a result, the fear is replaced by confidence.

At-Risk students must also be taught not to fear mistakes. Mistakes can be redefined as "learning experiences" quite necessary for growth--as long as they learn from them instead of giving away their POWER TO LEARN by making excuses or blaming someone else. By taking positive risks, they expand their Comfort Zone, which increases their freedom to act without fear!

At-risk students usually think that they have no control over what will happen to them in life, and that is why they initially resist the concept of setting goals; they believe it is simply wanted energy. We teach them that it is the job of the brain to create in reality whatever directions you give it through goal-setting as long as you BELIEVE it will happen and take the necessary steps. We also teach that those who regularly spend time *seeing themselves succeeding* greatly increase their chances of success. Athletes practice *seeing* themselves making the basket or the touchdown, because they know that this type of "mental practice", called visualization, is very effective. Our actions follow what we think about; if we constantly think of ourselves achieving our goals, we are actually "programming" our computer-brain for success.

This is but a part of the *PERSONAL DEVELOPMENT* curriculum, but the summary covers the philosophy and some of the most important concepts as they relate to the theme of EMPOWERING DISCIPLINE. Assertive communication skills, stress reduction, anger management strategies, and conflict resolution techniques are covered as well.

Of course, At-Risk students don't learn by being lectured to! Throughout the curriculum, I have used a lot of variety to hold the attention of the students. Large and small group discussions, worksheets, journal-writing, role plays, real-life case studies, poems, analogies, games, etc., are all balanced to prevent student boredom and encourage active involvement. The curriculum is scripted and uses a critical thinking approach where the teacher poses more questions than answers, and the students get to do most of the talking; but the questions are structured in such a way that the answers elicited support the lesson objectives. In the next Chapter we will discuss in depth the learning style of these students, as well as how we can structure classes so they will be motivated to do their best. I attempted to practice what I preach in the curriculum!

DESIGNING A CLASSROOM WHICH IS STRUCTURED FOR SUCCESS

The Second **D** of Empowering Discipline is designing a classroom which is structured so that your at-risk students can be successful. It is one thing to look for and encourage strengths in your students. It is another thing to create the environment whereby these students can *experience* these strengths for themselves. Empowering Discipline is based upon the realization that discipline problems develop when students *aren't* motivated, and that in order to *be* motivated, students must have some hope of success.

At-Risk youth find frustration rather than success in the way most classrooms are structured and in the way most subjects are taught. Remember, what brings *joy* to teachers with the personality temperament most typical in mainstream education *stresses* the typical at-risk learner. Likewise, the majority of at-risk youth come from the personality temperament whose joys represent stressors to the largest group of classroom teachers. The SJ teacher believes in planning, sequential teaching, step-by-step instructions, following the rules, work before pleasure, obedience, and responsibility. The SP student believes in trying to make work fun, learns best from unplanned, spontaneous, random, and kinesthetic experiences, and prefers self-directed learning and being creative. The typical secondary teacher uses the lecture-discussion method up to 70% of the time; the typical at-risk learner does *not* learn by listening.

I really liked an analogy I learned from Dr. Linda Berens of Temperament Research Institute in Huntington Beach, CA. She said that the typical class is taught like a marching band is organized. The teacher is up front, directing everything that is going on, and everyone is playing their instruments in a predetermined way, all in unison, and all marching in step under the watchful direction of the band director. The typical SP student is more like a talented jazz musician, who doesn't quite know *what* he is going to play until he hears the musician who is playing before him, at which point he will improvise upon the theme in some way. It is very difficult for a true jazz musician to function in a marching band--and vice versa. The jazz musician's strengths of creativity, spontaneity, and ability to improvise and create on the spot would not be honored in such a setting and, in fact, would be seen as insubordination!

Let's look once again at the characteristics of typical at-risk students as they relate to classroom instruction:

✓ They dislike feeling controlled or told what they *have* to do;
✓ They are discouraged with school;
✓ They don't like to do homework;
✓ They miss a lot of school;
✓ They need routine and structure but don't like it;
✓ They have short attention spans, get bored easily, and like excitement, action, and change;
✓ They dislike learning anything that is abstract and doesn't relate to their lives.
✓ They are competitive, like challenges, and want to show off and have fun.

No wonder these students become frustrated in mainstream classes! How can you teach students like this? I saw this message on a Tee-shirt at an alternative education conference:

If they
don't learn
the way we teach,
why don't we teach
the way they
learn?

If you are worried about how you can accomodate students who learn in a style so different from the way you teach, it will be comforting to know that students don't *have* to be taught in their style all the time. In fact, Dr. Bernice McCarthy (4-Mat) once told about her experience with an experiment whereby some students were paired with teachers who taught in their style *all the time,* some students were paired with teachers who taught in their style *none of the time,* and other students were paired with teachers who taught in their style *some of the time.* The students who did the best were those in the last group, where the teacher taught in a variety of styles, including the students' styles. By teaching in their style, the teacher *validated* them and gave them a chance to shine. Then these students were willing to be s-t-r-e-t-c-h-e-d the rest of the time. Those who were *always* taught in their style were never stretched. And those who were *never* taught in their style simply gave up!

It should come as no surprise that at-risk students are discouraged with school. If they are rarely taught in their style, they don't realize that they have any strengths. They see themselves being compared on a bell-shaped curve with students who *are* usually taught in their style, and they see themselves as lacking. They don't realize that they also have strengths that other students might lack. (Some *know* they're not stupid and think that what the school *teaches* is stupid! This might be the "healthier" attitude!)

I like to ask my workshop audiences: "If you had to choose

between being STUPID, or UNMOTIVATED, or a DISCIPLINE PROBLEM, which would you choose?" I rarely find a teacher who would choose to be STUPID. A few would choose to be UNMOTIVATED. But the biggest group--and these are teachers!-- say that they would choose to become DISCIPLINE PROBLEMS! This is the same choice our students are making. The solution isn't to "control" and "punish" them but to help them feel competent!

The best way to help them feel competent is to teach to their strengths at least part of the time. I am often asked how much time is "part of the time." I usually answer 25%, since there are four temperaments and I believe in Equal Educational Opportunity! But if you have primarily at-risk students in your classes, you will want a higher percentage than that spent in their style. More is usually better! Think of the students as consumers. If they don't want to "buy" it, many choose not to come!

By giving these students an opportunity to make a positive impact, you are giving yourself more opportunities to stroke them for their successes. Since they are discouraged, they need lots of C.P.R.--not the "mouth-to-mouth" kind--rather, **C**onstant **P**ositive **R**einforcement! Encouragement is the best reward: "Way to go; I *knew* you could do it!"

Next, use a SUCCESS ORIENTATION: Let them go at their own pace. Educators are always talking about "standards." It is not enough to have high standards if you are not helping all students *achieve* these standards. Start them with something *easy* to get their confidence up. You can increase the difficulty level *after* you have them hooked. Mark what is *right,* not what is wrong. Nothing is more discouraging to an already discouraged student than to receive a paper back covered with red check marks. Why should he bother to try if he is simply going to receive back further proof that he can't measure up.

It's not that you are going to overlook mistakes. You can use them diagnostically in order to determine what you need to teach that student or a group of students. And if you mark something right, you guarantee that the student will repeat it! Use FACE-SAVING STRATEGIES. At-risk students tend to over-react to criticism since they have faced so much of it. Use the *sandwich method*. Start with a positive, add a way to "make it even better" and end with a positive. Work on sounding non-judgmental and encouraging.

Most important, I believe, is getting rid of the BELL-SHAPED CURVE! Students will *remain* discouraged if their performance is always compared with the same straight A, college-bound group. If you wish to build motivation, have each student compete only with himself. Grade your students based upon their effort and improvement, not based upon a comparison with other students. My own District was always concerned about this point. If a "slow learner" could get an "A," what was to keep him or her from getting admitted to the University of California at Berkeley or to Stanford? My answer is that I have worked with thousands of at-risk students, and I have *never* had a student apply to either school. Therefore I think it is a bogus argument. If we want to motivate these students, we have to stop discouraging them when they really try and make significant improvement.

A second characteristic of at-risk students is that they want to be *SELF-DIRECTED* and do things their *own way*. We can work with this, but only if we stop seeing it as a sign of *disobedience!* We can *help* them be *better* at being self-directed by putting them in charge of their own educational programs and giving them choices. If you give them only *one* choice, the only choice they have is *not* to do what you say. Use their need to be autonomous instead of fighting it. Let them do their assignments their own unique way. Talk to them about their learning style and what seems to work best for them. Give them opportunities to make points by doing special projects in their learning style, and include projects that are *active* as some of the homework options.

I mentioned points. Points serve not only as external reinforcers; they also serve as a structure which holds a diversified classroom together. I discovered points out of necessity when I took over my school many years ago. Students seemed to go as slowly as possible. I asked several why everyone proceeded at such a snail's pace. They responded, "We're not stupid. If we get done with one book, the teacher will simply give us another one!" The game was to do as little as possible and still get credit for having worked that class period.

So we changed the game, giving five points for doing what the teacher would expect from each student during the fifty minute period. If the student got twice as much work done as was expected, he/she would get *ten* points. In contrast, if very little work was accomplished, the student might receive one or two points, if any. We were an alternative school, so we could give variable credits, but I have found that this same system also works just as well in semester systems without variable credit. The points simply determine the grade.

You can therefore tell your students that in your class, they can CHOOSE THEIR OWN GRADE! You can challenge them to try for an "A"! Ask how long it has been since they have received one, and then suggest that they might want to take up a wager with a parent by asking, "What would you give me if I got an 'A' in English (or in Math or Science or Social Studies)?" Then share with your students your system concerning how many points it takes for an "A", a "B", a "C", etc.

Once you have established a point system, you can open up yet other options that put the students in charge of their own educational programs. Instead of homework being *mandatory* (which almost *always* guarantees that at-risk students won't do it!), it can be presented as an *opportunity* to make *extra* points, outside of teacher supervision! We made it even more desirable by *not allowing it* at first, until the student had established a good pattern of attendance and classroom participation! We'd simply say that we were not a correspondence school, and that our funding wasn't based on the work they did at home. If they didn't come to school, we wouldn't have the funds to run our program. (Students who had refused to do homework for years suddenly wanted it and would become incensed when told they had to first "earn" the right for it!)

Points also open up the opportunity to give OPTIONAL TESTS. You can offer periodic optional tests which students don't *have* to take but for which they can earn, say, twenty points for an "A", fifteen points for a "B", or ten points for a "C". Then you can offer the option of bringing a "cheat sheet", as long as it measures no larger than 3" X 5." Do you realize how much studying a student must do to figure out what might be asked in order to squeeze the correct answers on such a small cheat sheet?! Make sure the students understand that they will get only half the number of points if they choose to use a cheat sheet. Then, the day of the test, you can challenge them to try to *double* their points by not using their cheat sheets! Meanwhile, you have "tricked" them into studying for a test, something they wouldn't ordinarily do!

You can give them choices even when it comes to test questions. At-risk students generally don't do as well with essay tests, as they tend to be concrete, not abstract, in their thinking. So you can give them a choice of doing either two out of three essay questions or, say, twenty out of thirty objective questions. If they elect to do *more* of the questions than called for, give them extra points. Or tell them that if they learned something that you forgot to ask, to write about that for extra points (which you will determine based on the value of the information). Always give students the option of taking an oral test. Some students learn a lot but have a very hard time expressing what they know in writing, and some are test-phobic and freeze up.

By structuring your classes this way, you can work with your students to help them set their *own* goals. What grade do they plan to earn? Or in the case of variable credit classes, how long do they want to spend in the class? How fast do they want to proceed through their program? And even, when do they plan to graduate-- *with their* class or the following year or the year after that? And, how many credits will they have to earn per month in order to achieve their goal? Then you become the ally, the advocate, the coach, the one who can gently remind a student that you remember that she had wanted an 'A', but that you figured her points last night. "Would you like to know how they came out?....No, at the current rate you'll end up with a D-. Is that okay with you, or would you like to know some things you can do to pick up your pace?" With this kind of atmosphere, the at-risk student, who isn't being told what he *must do*, is much more likely to make good choices. Besides, these students tend to be very egalitarian in nature, and they react much better to this kind of problem-solving, "adult-to-adult" approach.

You often hear mainstream educators repeat a variation of this:

Students need
a *predictable* environment,
clear boundaries, and
the *expectation* that
they will be *responsible.*

I agree with this statement, but only if we can add the following:

Within the boundaries,
students need
choices and control
over what they do.

You control the environment.
Let the students *control*
themselves.

What you are doing is *using* their need for control by putting them *in charge of* their own educational program. Motivation grows out of a sense of feeling "in charge." (And remember, it is this sense of feeling "in charge" that builds resiliency!) This approach is a non-coercive, non-confrontational, and non-adversarial one. At workshops, I like to use the MacDonalds' example. If someone approached a trained counter clerk at MacDonalds and said "I *don't* want a Big Mac!", the clerk wouldn't be expected to overpower the customer and insist that he or she order what is good enough for millions of customers all over the country (and around the world!). The clerk would simply suggest several other options. This is the approach to use when a student adamantly expresses his or her distaste for a certain assignment. It doesn't *have* to become a test of wills and a potential disciplinary incident. You can simply help the student examine the other options available. And, like at Mac-Donalds, the options aren't unlimited. (But if MacDonalds only had one choice on its menu, as many classes do, they probably would not be in business today!)

It is important to make sure that the "classroom management system" you create provides the proper balance of incentives (to motivate students) and built-in pressures (or many at-risk students will go too slow). What all do you need? We have talked about the first two of the components, all of which are listed below:

(1) GIVE CHOICES to *empower* your students and put them in charge of their educational goals. This changes your role to that of coach or ally, who is helping them define and achieve their goals instead of someone who is telling them what to do.

(2) AWARD POINTS for work accomplished. This provides an incentive along with teaching cause and effect, which many at-risk students haven't grasped yet. (The harder they work, the more points they will earn, and the higher their grade or the greater the number of credits they will earn. It is up to them.)

45

(3) <u>DESIGN POINT CATEGORIES</u>. This way the "system" will guide their choices. Without point categories, students might choose all their assignments from a favorite category and end up with an unbalanced program. *With* point categories, you can gently remind a student that she has almost "used up" all of her points from that category and help her make different choices.

(4) <u>PROVIDE GRADING CHECKPOINTS</u>. At-risk students tend to put off work until the deadline. By having regular checkpoints, or even by giving grades every three weeks or so and then averaging the grades to come up with the semester grade, you are having the system create "pressure" on a regular basis. Then you can provide the support necessary to help the student be successful within the system.

(5) <u>PROVIDE INTRINSIC MOTIVATION</u>. When students are taught the way they are wired to learn and when they are taught things which are of interest to them and meet their needs, *intrinsic* motivation occurs quite naturally. Teachers often complain that at-risk students lack (intrinsic) motivation. This is not surprising when you consider how few teachers there are who teach the way these students learn! Whenever students (of any personality temperament) are not taught in their style, they will lose intrinsic motivation. You can increase the intrinsic motivation of at-risk students by making the lessons fun, hands-on and active, challenging and competitive, and related to their interests, needs, and real life problems.

(6) <u>CREATE EXTRINSIC INCENTIVES</u>. Extrinsic motivation is often criticized as unnecessary by those who believe knowledge should always be its own reward. It is, but primarily to one personality temperament, the NT's, who make up just 6% of the students! In addition, SJ's learn because they are *supposed* to, and NF's tend to like learning and generally

want to please, so these students will usually learn even in an environment lacking in extrinsic incentives. But SP's are wired to want a payoff! And, as pointed out above, few teachers naturally teach in a way that provides SP's with *intrinsic* motivation. I look at this in a practical way. Extrinsic incentives give students something to focus on besides misbehavior and help provide a goal to aim for. By providing a "payoff", you are "jump-starting" them into action, at least at first, until the feeling of "success" hopefully *becomes* its own reward.

To get at-risk students motivated, you've got to provide incentives that matter to them--and **emphasize the incentives more than negative consequences or punishments**. With these students, the **carrot** works much better than the **stick**! At-risk students won't do things because they *have* to do them--only because they *want* to do them. We need to be *persuasive* as well as *creative* in our use of incentives. Points are an excellent form of extrinsic motivation. Other incentives can be *anything* a student wants which you can link to what *you* need from them first (e.g.-- "You can work on the computer as soon as you finish your assignment" or "You can sit together as long as you work quietly.") Then, if they fail to fulfill their part of the bargain, you don't have to "punish", you simply remove the incentive.

You can also formalize incentives into an entire system of levels, with different privileges involved at each level. This works best where there is a "level playing field", where students compete only against themselves. In a class based upon the bell-shaped curve, at-risk students would simply not aspire to any of the higher levels because they would not see any hope of making it. In fact, their behavior might actually deteriorate. Their thinking would likely be, "If I don't have a chance to succeed, I am going to be the very best at being the *worst* I can be!"

We've talked about the type of structure which best motivates at-risk students; now let's talk about the type of instruction that is most appealing and effective, again reviewing the characteristics of this type of learner. First, they have **short attention spans, get bored easily, and like excitement, action, and change**. To put this a more positive way, they pay attention to *everything,* so nothing holds their attention for long. They need a highly stimulating environment to catch and hold their attention, so you have to be creative to keep them focused. The view *used* to be that these students needed a bland environment so they wouldn't get distracted. However, this approach would simply put them to sleep. Now we know that they need MORE, not less, stimulation to keep them interested and awake!

What is the solution? **Provide variety!** (This goes without saying if you have students with different learning styles in your room anyway but also applies if you have all SP's!) Keep any group instruction vivid and fast-paced, switching modalities regularly. Remember, these are ACTIVE, KINESTHETIC learners. They need to be DOING something, not just sitting passively and listening, as is the case with much of large group instruction. I once heard that the problem with schools is that they are places where *young people* go to watch *old people* work, and it should be the other way around!

These students are also WHOLE-TO PART-LEARNERS. You need to help them see the BIG PICTURE first, before they care about or can hold onto any of the details. This is why they often get bogged down doing individual reading. They can't seem to find the big picture as they struggle with all the individual words. You can help them by explaining the overall theme or what they should be looking for, and also by teaching them such study skills as pre-reading the headings and the chapter questions first. If students are each working out of different books so that there are too many themes to be explained, challenge them to "speed-read" the first time they confront new material, looking only for the BIG PICTURE and ignoring all details. They can pick up the details the second time through. Explain that this will save them time in the long run.

Some teachers of at-risk youth prefer an entirely individualized approach, so that students will each be able to proceed at their own pace and so that the teacher can provide individual attention to students as needed. Other teachers prefer group instruction, because these students become bored reading and need stimulation. My own view is that the best approach is to alternate the two approaches. At-risk youth need the stimulation which can't be provided so easily with an individualized approach. But they also get frustrated being part of a group for long periods of time without being able to do "their own thing." When they become uptight over being part of a "marching band" type of class, they often start to sabotage the class, just to get a sense of their own efficacy.

I think it is best to start with a short group activity to gain everyone's attention, to provide "set", and to create interest and motivation. Follow this group activity with students doing related assignments of their own choosing which are related to the theme. This gives students the opportunity to proceed at their own pace, earning points as they go, and it gives you the time you will need to work with and to encourage individual students. At-risk students tend to get discouraged and will attempt to "talk themselves out of trying" on a regular basis. They need you to notice this and to intervene, perhaps through a "point check" or a quick pep talk! If you are doing whole group instruction all of the time, you won't be able to provide this type of one-on-one intervention.

Although at-risk students like variety, they tend not to handle transitions well, perhaps because it is the teacher calling the shots and changing the pace. So be sure to let them know ahead of time what will be happening, and use points when necessary to drive the direction you want them to go. (For example, if you want students to participate in an important activity you think they will resist, give them the choice, but give double points to everyone who chooses the activity instead of doing their ongoing individual assignments.)

Computers, multimedia, the Internet, and video are perfect for the way that kinesthetic students learn. They see technology as toys! Computers especially give them a sense of focus and control, since what is going on in a good software program, especially a colorful, interactive program which gives immediate feedback, seems more exciting that what is going on around them! When word processing is used, students' printed work, especially if a spell-checker and a good font are used, can look very "professional", at least compared to their usually poor handwriting! (Most seem to write like doctors!) And when mistakes are made, they are so simple to correct by highlighting, correcting and then reprinting. I have seen students who formerly didn't care about their work become almost obsessed with getting it "perfect", especially if the result was going to be "published" in a student "literary journal" or newspaper being produced by the class.

One of my teachers captured his students' need to be active by having them "make" short movies using multimedia. They would write the script and select the pictures from a hypercard stack, and then record a narration of the script in sync with the pictures. I also knew of a teacher who had his students design their own websites. Their web pages would become their student portfolios for their "very best work!" Then he could always ask, "Do you think that assignment is good enough yet to be included on your web pages?"

My view on videos is that students have become so jaded due to the hours of television most watch that the showing of videos *can* lead to a very passive form of learning. My suggestion is that the viewing of videos be in segments of about ten minutes, with short discussions about the content before proceeding to the next segment.

Another option is to have worksheets that students can fill out as they watch if they wish to receive any points.

Another characteristic of at-risk youth is that they tend to be **practical, concrete, and want education to relate to their lives.** So, look for ways to relate what you are teaching to their lives in some way. They seem to learn on a "need to know" basis; when they need to know, they will figure out where to find the information. Unless you can figure out a way to relate the information to your students' lives in some way, they probably won't learn it. Career Math and Real-Life Math will appeal to these students much more than algebra. Teaching writing by using as pre-writing exercises readings which cover problems that the students themselves face will be much more effective than using the classics to stimulate writing. We found that reading scores went up and writing skills improved when we started using the *COPING CURRICULUM* series from the Rosen Corporation to stimulate thinking before giving related writing assignments. Students loved these books because they dealt with real problems they faced. This need for relevance is also why it is so important to use multi-cultural learning materials. Minority students need to see that the education they are receiving relates in some way to *their* lives.

Projects which have some purpose solving **real-world problems** will be much more appealing to at-risk youth than the learning of information for its own sake, especially when the projects involve **doing** something. Students like to **make an impact upon their environment.** Examples include a Health or Social Studies class which is studying drug abuse competing at writing skits dissuading younger children from getting involved with drug use, with the winning skit or skits being allowed to perform at a local elementary (or middle) school; or mock trials in Social Studies involving historical persons and events. One science class studied stream ecology and then had the students raise trout from the egg stage and later release them into local streams (amid much positive publicity!).

At-risk students tend to like **competition**, **challenges**, and **fun**. Cooperative learning teams can be formed to compete against one another (for fun, learning, and the building of relationships!). Use competition to make drill work and review more exciting, using relays, games, and puzzles. Simulations and role-playing can be used, when appropriate, to enliven a lesson, and these activities give SP's their chance to show off their **spontaneity** and **creativity**. They love to **perform** and share their **cleverness!** Also, have the class plan special activities for special holidays. Get everyone involved. This does not represent a wasted day for learning. Many students, who learn more by **doing**, learn a great deal through such extra-curricular activities. Anything which keeps at-risk students coming to school represents a big plus!

Sometimes you will try a new activity which you expect that students will really like and they will complain that it is BORING! Don't take it personally. Many at-risk students are so used to complaining about classroom activities that it becomes almost a habit! Ask them to please humor you. If they continue to complain, simply have a very boring backup activity or worksheet which you can have them do instead. After you have used this strategy several times, if anyone complains about one of your activities being boring, the other students will over-rule him or her!

Some at-risk students will be reluctant to participate in some activities because they fear failure or don't want to risk looking foolish if they do poorly in front of their peers. They are the ones who need to build hope. Keep supporting and encouraging them. When you design group activities, always provide some "passive" roles, such as observer. Not everyone has to volunteer to role-play, for example. Allow those who are reluctant to be among the "audience" for awhile. You can encourage them privately to take a more active role in time, perhaps offering bonus points for taking a risk and *s-t-r-e-t-c-h-i-n-g!* And when a student seems stressed, you can always give him the choice of skipping group participation on a given day and doing his individual assignment instead.

Another thing which will happen when you start making changes in the way you teach is that students who had previously been happy with the way things *were*--those whose style you had mainly been teaching to--will start to complain! There is no lesson which will please *all* students. But Equal Educational Opportunity calls for giving each learning style its turn! In other words, rotate who is unhappy! If the same students are *always* unhappy, their learning style and strengths are probably not being highlighted. Give them their day to shine. Console students who don't like a specific strategy by letting them know that whenever they *don't* enjoy the way you are teaching, they are *S-T-R-E-T-C-H-I-N-G!*

Howard Gardner's theory of MULTIPLE INTELLIGENCES can be of help to you as you select strategies which will be appropriate to your at-risk students. I especially like Thomas Armstrong's book *MULTIPLE INTELLIGENCES IN THE CLASSROOM,* published by ASCD. Armstrong was a learning disabilities specialist who became frustrated with the "deficit-oriented" paradigm in Special Education. He could see that many of his supposedly "disabled" students were clearly gifted in other areas. He discovered Howard Gardner's theory of Multiple Intelligences and spent eight years applying this theory to the nuts-and-bolts issues of classroom teaching, resulting in the above book.

I have outlined on pages 55 and 56 the seven intelligences and the strategies which Armstrong says best express each type of intelligence (and often help develop it in those who are not strong in it). I would like to suggest that you use the list of activities like you would use a Food Group list! To get a balanced meal, you would choose foods from *each* of the Food Groups, and not serve a meal where every item is from the Dairy Products Food Group!

As an alternative to sequenced instruction, which isn't a natural learning style for most at-risk learners, you can do the following:

✓ Choose a broad relevant theme.

✓ Choose the supporting activities in a balanced way from all of the MI categories, alternating group and individualized instruction as mentioned earlier.

✓ Provide **CHOICES**.

✓ Use a point system to provide external reinforcement and to assist recordkeeping and grading.

✓ Make it **relevant, fun, vivid,** and **varied.** And realize that **emotion aids retention!**

To best reach your at-risk students, especially incorporate strategies from the **Spatial, Bodily-Kinesthetic, Musical, Interpersonal, and Intrapersonal Intelligence** categories. At-risk learners tend to have talents in one or more of these areas. Perhaps they are at-risk in our schools because their strengths do not tend to lie in the two types of intelligence which we emphasize and which standardized tests measure--Linguistic and Logical-Mathematical. Also incorporate strategies from the second bullet listed under Linguistic intelligence (**Brainstorming, Story-telling, Journal writing, tape recording, student publishing**.) Armstrong highly recomends these strategies as they will help develop linguistic intelligence in those who aren't strong in it.

There are a number of programs which I'd like to mention that work extremely well with at-risk students. They each place students in real-life situations where they begin to discover strengths they didn't know they had. These programs also help students develop aspirations for the future as they start to see themselves differently.

MULTIPLE INTELLIGENCES

1. **LINGUISTIC INTELLIGENCE**--(Word Smart: Read, write, and talk about it)

   - Lectures, discussions, books, worksheets (Used 70% of time by teachers, but these techniques reach only a segment of learners)
   - Brainstorming, Storytelling, Journal writing, tape recording, student publishing (All are highly recommended by Armstrong as they will help develop linguistic intelligence in *all* learners.)
   - Word processing, individualized reading, debating, word games

2. **LOGICAL-MATHEMATICAL INTELLIGENCE** (Number Smart or Logic Smart: Quantify it, think critically about it, conceptualize it)

   - Logical-sequential presenting of subject matter
   - Math problems on board
   - Scientific demonstrations
   - Logic puzzles, games
   - Socratic Questioning approach
   - Critical thinking

3. **SPATIAL INTELLIGENCE**--(Picture Smart: See it, draw it, visualize it, color it, mind-map it)

   - Videos, slides, movies, photography
   - Art appreciation
   - Painting, collage, visual arts
   - Charts, graphs, maps, diagrams, puzzles
   - Visualization
   - Imaginative storytelling
   - Visual metaphors
   - Mind-mapping and other visual organizers
   - Computer graphics
   - Color coding of material
   - Sketching of concepts (Pictionary)

4. **BODILY-KINESTHETIC INTELLIGENCE**-(Body Smart: Build it, act it out, touch it, get a "gut-feeling, dance it)

- Field trips
- Physical education activities
- Physical relaxation activities
- Classroom drama/improvisations
- Games
- Crafts
- Cooking, gardening, etc.
- Use of manipulatives, lab work

5. **MUSICAL INTELLIGENCE**-(Music Smart: Sing it, rap it, listen to it)

- Singing, playing live or recorded music
- Linking old tunes with concepts
- Music appreciation
- Using background music
- Using rhythms, songs, raps, and chants

6. **INTERPERSONAL INTELLIGENCE**-(People Smart: Teach it, collaborate on it)

- Cooperative learning
- Peer teaching, cross-age tutoring
- Conflict mediation
- Group brainstorming
- Community involvement; Apprenticeships; Community Service
- Simulations
- Board games

7. **INTRAPERSONAL INTELLIGENCE**-(Self-Smart: Connect it to your own life, make choices connected with it)

- Independent Study
- Self-paced instruction, individualized projects
- Giving choices; options
- One-minute reflection periods
- Motivational curricula and self-esteem activities
- Goal-setting activities
- Journal keeping
- Connecting content with students' own lives
- Infusing content with emotion

These programs include the following:

- ⇨ PEER TUTORING AND CROSS-AGE TUTORING
- ⇨ COMMUNITY SERVICE
- ⇨ SERVICE LEARNING
- ⇨ TEACHING OF PRO-SOCIAL SKILLS, ATTITUDES
- ⇨ COMMUNITY-SCHOOL COLLABORATION
- ⇨ ADVENTURE EDUCATION
- ⇨ MENTORING
- ⇨ YOUTH EMPLOYMENT
- ⇨ CAREER EDUCATION
- ⇨ ACADEMIES AND SCHOOLS WITHIN SCHOOLS

Whenever you place at-risk youth in a situation where they are helping others, they realize that they *do* have something to give. As a result, they feel less "needy." They start to develop a sense of altruism and empathy which might have been lacking before. They start thinking about their futures. **Peer tutoring, cross-age tutoring, community service**, and **service learning** are especially helpful in this regard.

We sent our at-risk high school students to the County's one week Science Camp to be the Cabin Leaders for the fifth and sixth grade campers. We were told that our students did a better job than the Honor Students from the comprehensive high schools! We sent more students to Science camp over a four year period than any other school in the County. I think camp did *our* students more good than it did the fifth and sixth graders! They came back *changed*. They loved the experience and talked for weeks about everything that had happened. Many would answer letters they received from their campers and seemed amazed that they were so *admired!* Some would start asking questions about what it took to become a teacher. Most started to do better in school. Almost all wanted to return for another week!

Such experiences also lead to **the teaching of pro-social attitudes and skills**. Suddenly students "needed to know" such "parenting" skills as how to handle a stubborn young camper who refused to participate in a required part of the camping program. It was always fun hearing students talk about "how bad" some of the campers had been; it certainly caused them to look at *our* roles differently!

Community-School collaboration can result in the creation of programs for students that no separate organization could handle alone. Such collaboration can also result in increased opportunities to be awarded grant money, as collaboration counts for many points in the scoring of grant applications. Perhaps highly experiential **Adventure Education** programs such as Outward Bound or ROPES course outings can be funded that way.

Mentoring programs have grown in popularity and are now even recommended by the White House. At-risk youth need as many positive role models as we can provide for them! Sometimes mentors can be found from a career area which a student is interested in. **Career Education** and **Youth Employment** programs are both critical. Too many youth simply cannot visualize themselves as adults and have been convinced that there *is* no future for them. Without aspirations, students won't make the sacrifices necessary to be successful. I especially like John Holland's Self-Directed Search career test (from Psychological Assessment Resources, Inc., Odessa, FL). I also like *DO WHAT YOU ARE* by the Tiegers, a book which looks at careers according to personality type. Review some of the careers which are appropriate for SP's which follows. Talk about them with your students and look for matches between interests and possible careers. Once a student has something to lose, he or she is much more likely to make responsible choices!

SOME SP CAREERS

Firefighter	Surveyor
Detective/Investigator	Retail Sales
Coach	Licensed Voc. Nurse
Car Sales	Veterinarian
Contractor	Flight Attendant
Stockbroker	Film Producer
Aircraft Mechanic	Fitness Instrutor
Marine Biologist	Art Therapist
Land Developer	Travel Agent
Real Estate Sales	Fashion Designer
Sportscaster	Geologist
News Reporter	Forester
Profess. Athlete	Carpenter
Insurance Broker	Commercial Artist

Academies and **schools within schools** are good for at-risk youth as well because of their generally smaller size and supportive staff. Academies are usually career-related. Students enroll voluntarily because of a career interest shared by all students in that academy. All of their mainstream classes are taught from the perspective of that career interest. This is *not* tracking because the career interests are broadly defined. A Health Academy, for example, can include careers ranging from doctor through nurses' aide. Other examples of academies include a Performing Arts Academy, a Hospitality and Tourism Academy, a Business Careers Academy, an Oceanography Academy, etc. (One caution: Although academies are perfect for at-risk students, some districts, such as my own, in effect prevent at-risk students from participating by requiring that applicants be totally caught up on their credits. I feel that a certain percentage of slots--say, twenty percent--should be held open for students who would not otherwise qualify but who show special talents or potential for success in the academy.)

In summary, we can *prevent* many of the disciplinary problems in our classrooms by building positive, supportive relationships with our students, by teaching them the attitudes and skills which will help them access their inner resilience, and by creating an environment in which they can flourish. Such an environment is one where their **d**iverse talents can be **d**iscovered, **d**eveloped, and **d**isplayed! (More **D's**!) This involves *all* teachers going outside their own teaching style part of the time to teach in ways that aren't natural for them in order to reach students whose learning style is *different* from their own. As we look to the 21st Century, we need to recognize that *all* students will benefit from activities which encourage spontaneity and adapting quickly to change. And finally:

Most
At-Risk students
learn best when the material
is made PERSONALLY MEANINGFUL
and when they are ACTIVELY INVOLVED
and given CHOICES, VARIETY, and
ENCOURAGEMENT in a
POSITIVE CLIMATE
where they feel
VALUED
& have
FUN!

SP LEARNING STYLE (Concrete-Random)[2]

SP learners prefer non-structured spontaneous activities which are action-oriented, fun, and exciting. They like hands-on projects which have a practical real-world application. They learn by doing and need immediate feedback. They enjoy competition, having to improvise, and being the center of attention. They need to be given the opportunity to show off their talents at being spontaneous and clever. They also need to use their sense of humor to keep from getting bored.

Sometimes their spontaneity and sense of humor cause them problems in traditional classrooms, as they often cause disruptions in class by calling attention to themselves. However, they can be won over as an "ally" if reinforced for the "excitement" they bring to class and for their potential leadership skills (which need refining!). Other stressors for SP's involve too much routine, having to wait, too many rules, and strict time limits. They need to have variety in their learning activities because sameness causes them to lose interest. They also need an open seating arrangement and freedom to move about, hands-on activities, competition, games, improvs and an action-oriented approach, as much as possible. They prefer to do any assignments in their own original and non-traditional style. This group is most at-risk in traditional educational settings. Many are in alternative schools or have dropped out.

SP's LEARN BECAUSE IT'S FUN OR BECAUSE THEY NEED THE INFORMATION TO GET SOMETHING RELATED TO THEIR GOALS DONE RIGHT NOW!

---

[2] See page 100 for information on the "Other" Three Learning Styles, based upon both Keirsey's Personality Temperment Theory and Gregorc's model.

WAYS TO HELP SP's LEARN
A Summary Double Check ✓✓

✓ Be POSITIVE, ENCOURAGING, and RESPECTFUL.

✓ BE SUCCESS ORIENTED: Let them go at own pace.

✓ GIVE CHOICES--so they feel "in charge."

✓ Use EXTERNAL MOTIVATORS (especially points).

✓ Use SHORT-TERM ASSIGNMENTS + "allow special projects" for makeup points or "extra credit" (instead of calling it "homework"). Give immediate feedback.

✓ Frequently change gears and provide VARIETY.

✓ ALTERNATE group and individualized instruction.

✓ LIMIT DISTRACTIONS and use VISUAL AIDS. Be VIVID!

✓ Always teach a PRACTICAL application. Make it REAL!

✓ For anything too abstract, offer CONCRETE options.

✓ Incorporate EXPERIMENTS, VIDEOS, COMPUTERS.

✓ Whenever possible, MAKE LEARNING FUN! Use games, challenges, relays, puzzles, simulations, improvs.

✓ Give students legitimate opportunities to SHOW OFF.

✓ REINFORCE them for their SKILL, HUMOR, CLEVERNESS, SPONTANEITY.

✓ Use COMPETITION to make drill-work & review FUN!

DEFUSING
PROBLEM BEHAVIOR

I don't need to tell you that traditional disciplinary techniques don't work with most at-risk youth. You undoubtedly confront proof of this fact-of-life on a regular basis. We have already discussed why this is so, but let's review it again:

THEY DON'T WANT TO BE TOLD WHAT TO DO!

There is a line from a country song which Trisha Yearwood sings that I like to call the SP line:

> "I want to go too far;
> I want to go too fast.
> Somebody draw the line
> so I can *blow* right past!"

Remember, this attitude originates out of a need to be *self*-directed, not out of a need to be defiant. It is only when, with all of our good intentions we inadvertently *thwart* their need to be *self*-directed, that behavior escalates and can end up appearing to be defiance against our authority. We can keep it from reaching that point by carefully selecting responses which DEFUSE potential problems instead of escalating them. Control is always a major issue when working with these students, and it is how you address this issue that determines how successful you will be working with them.

So what can you do? The first step is to give up any illusion that you can control anyone who does not *want* to be controlled. If you wish to change student behavior, you first need to change the way you see your teacher "job description", transforming it in your mind into a role which is non-adversarial and supportive in nature. We can't really control anyone else anyway. All students have to say is "NO!" and they are back in control and one-up over us. So:

THE TEACHER'S JOB
is *not to*
CONTROL the students
but to
OFFER CHOICES
and GUIDANCE
to help them
get their needs met
in a POSITIVE WAY.

It helps to understand that students act up when their Basic Needs aren't met. Students have a need to belong, to feel competent, and to feel a sense of efficacy, or personal power, which students see tied up with RESPECT. When students misbehave, see it as a symptom and DECODE IT! What does it mean? What NEED is not being met? Fire extinguishers contain instructions that are appropriate for us to remember in this context as well:

"AIM THE HOSE AT THE *BASE* OF THE FLAMES!"

Student misbehavior is often the result of their feeling OVER-CONTROLLED. *MORE* control will simply escalate oppositional behavior. Instead of trying to *OVERPOWER* a disruptive student and attempting to force him to do what *you* want, you'll find that you will be far more successful if the student sees you as his ALLY, someone who is helping him (or her) figure out ways to achieve the power and respect he needs (although you will *not* describe the problem that way in talking with the student!).

Defusing problem behavior involves **Detaching** yourself emotionally, **Disengaging** yourself from any power struggle, and then **De-escalating** the crisis. You can resolve the problem at the Fourth step--the **Debriefing** stage. But this comes *later,* when the student (and perhaps you as well!) has calmed down, and most importantly when there is no longer an audience for the student to play to. There is no way that you can get an upset student to look at a situation differently if a group of his or her peers is watching!

The following is what you must tell yourself if you are to be successful during the Defusing stage. (It does *not* come naturally!):

I CAN'T control this student.
I don't WANT to control him.
I want to help him think
about HIS CHOICES.
I need to stay CALM,
POSITIVE, and
in control
of ME!

In other words, don't personalize; it's not *about you!* Aim for CARING DETACHMENT. You *care* about the student but you are not trying to *control* her behavior. Don't try to control the *outcome.* Just follow the *process* and tell yourself,

"NO MATTER WHAT HAPPENS, I CAN HANDLE IT!"

Remember, if you get into a power struggle with a student, you have surrendered control to the student, and you have therefore
LOST!

It is important to always be aware of your body language. Seventy percent of our communication is through our body language, so you might be inadvertently telling lots of things to students that you don't realize you are sharing! At-risk students are often very good at picking up on subtle non-verbal cues. Tone of voice contributes another 23 % to your communication. This leaves a mere 7% of communication conveyed by words! You might *think* you are simply "pointing out consequences" in order to help a student make a good decision, but if the student feels you are "threatening" him with the consequences, he will probably "lock into" his position or escalate it. It is important that you *not* act frustrated or angry, because that means the student is succeeding at pushing your buttons, and it will be hard for him to let that go! Remember, anger locks in attitudes. You do *not* want an angry attitude "locked in."

A teacher at a workshop shared with me an excellent example of how she dealt with a disruptive student in a non-disciplinarian way. This example illustrates three critical points: the importance of meeting a students needs, of not hooking in by becoming angry ourselves, and of monitoring our body language and tone of voice. The setting was a computer lab, where a student was acting out by walking around the room disrupting other students. When the teacher re-directed him to his seat, he began pushing several keys on the keyboard creating a continual irritating beep. The teacher realized that what the student needed at that moment was attention. So, she sat down next to him and began to help him and give him "positive energy". When the student asked the teacher what she was doing, she replied that she was giving him her undivided attention because that was what she thought he wanted. The teacher said that the student's behavior immediately changed and he began to do his assignment.

Sometimes, *what* you say isn't as important as the caring you project. Talking *softer*, not louder than the student, projecting *gentleness* rather than control, appearing *concerned* instead of angry--all of these strategies will be much more effective when your goal is to defuse student anger.

The way you talk with students must also enforce your *positive expectations*. If you *see* them in a positive way and *expect* them to make good choices, they really *will* act better! Be sure to always USE *PERMISSIVE LANGUAGE*--never restrictive language. For example, say

"You can...when..."

not

"You can't...until..."

"Can't" is often taken as a *CHALLENGE*. Say "You can come back to class as soon as your mom gives me a call", not "You can't come back to class until your mom calls me." Chances are that an at-risk student would respond, "I don't want to come back to your _____ class anyway!"

Remember to always be *PERSUASIVE*. Word what the student *has* to do in terms which connect with his needs. For example, if your school has a policy, as so many schools do, which require students who are late to go to the Office to get a tardy slip, don't say to a late student "You *have* to go to the Office to get a tardy slip." Say, "You'll *want* to go to the Office to let them know you're here so they won't call your home." The way you word things can make a BIG difference in the student's response.

When students ask you permission questions, always say "Yes", not "No", but then link the behavior you need as a condition. For example, say "Of course you can watch the video--as soon as you complete your assignment" *not* "No, you can't watch the video because you haven't finished your assignment." Use phrases like

"When you...then you can..." or

"If you...then you can..." or

"As soon as you...then you can..." or

"As long as you...then you can..."statements.

This sets conditions which are logical and have nothing to do with your controlling the student. (Bluestein, 1998)

Link the incentive students want with the boundaries.

In place of telling a student what he or she *has* to do, it is far more effective to *ASK* gentle *QUESTIONS*, *or* to *GIVE CHOICES*. To be effective at this, you have to ASSUME THE BEST and use supportive, or at least neutral, body language. See page 69 for some examples. These are all non-confrontational communications.

Often using *fewer* words works better, especially if the result sounds more like a "suggestion" than an order. If a student has a hat on, and your school has a "no-hat" rule, simply saying "Your hat?" and pointing to your head will be more effective than saying, "It's against the school rules to wear a hat in class. Please take it off." Likewise, if you want a student to sit down, saying "Your chair?" and pointing toward it can sound more like a friendly reminder than a direct command.

One thing to beware of is the warning which goes "*Next time* I see you talking to her..." That is a game called "GOTCHA," and most at-risk students will not respond well as they will think you are threatening them. Of *course* they won't be perfect! Instead, look for *effort* and reinforce *improvement* (e.g. "I noticed how hard you tried to keep from talking to Joe. I'll bet you do better tomorrow.")

Sometimes students will comply with your requests but will do

DON'T MAKE DEMANDS.
INSTEAD, (with a smile)...

(1) ASK QUESTIONS:

- "Do you need any help?
- "What do you plan to do?"
- "Do you think you can get as much work done if you sit together?"
- "Is that behavior appropriate?" or "Is that really necessary?" or "Could you save it for after class?"
- "What do you think will happen if you keep doing that?" (If they respond that they don't know, suggest: "You might want to think about it!")
- "Just because I *like* you, do you really think I should let you get away with that?" (From Fay and Funk, 1995)

(2) GIVE CHOICES (AND FOLLOW THROUGH IF THE STUDENT DOESN'T):

- "Do you know what you should be doing, or do you need me to review it with you?"
- "Do you think you can sit together quietly, or do you need to move to another seat?"
- "If you cooperate with me by moving today, we can try having you sit together again tomorrow. Or we can discuss it in the Office today. You choose."
- "Would you prefer to cool off here or somewhere else?"

(3) GIVE INFORMATION ABOUT WHAT YOU NEED:

- "I need everyone to listen carefully" not "You need to quiet down."
- "I need to get through, please" not "Could you please move?"

(4) TELL THEM WHAT YOU'LL DO, NOT WHAT THEY MUST DO:

- "I'll be happy to listen when you can talk respectfully."
- "I'll be happy to see you back in class after we've had a chance to talk privately. When would be best?"

it with a negative attitude. Let's say that you had agreed that two students could study together as long as they worked quietly, and then they failed to live up to their end of the bargain. Obviously, you need to follow through and have them move to separate seats. Once again you can link an incentive to a boundary by suggesting that if they *cooperate* with you today, you'll agree that they can try sitting together again tomorrow. Let's suppose they *do* move, but with an *attitude*. Perhaps they roll their eyes or sigh, or mumble something to themselves, or move slowly with exaggerated movements.

I have found that the best response is to thank them for complying and to ignore the attitude, at least right then, (unless it is *so* extreme that it is a downright defiance of authority) because otherwise things will probably escalate. You might want to add, "My, you are *so dramatic!*" to the "Thank you." Then, the next morning you can ask to speak with them privately, and add your need for them to be "less dramatic" as part of the condition to their being able to sit together again. "I'd really like to give you another chance to work together, because I *do* think you'd do better today, but I need to know two things: First, that you would talk together a lot less than you did yesterday--and more quietly, and second, that if I *do* need to ask you to move, that you would be far less dramatic and move without calling any attention to yourselves. Do you think you can do that, or would you rather just take separate seats?"

Speaking to students privately like this, especially if you use a pleasant, positive, and supportive tone, usually brings about a much better response than entering into an argument with them with the class watching. I can't emphasize this enough. Some issues simply need to be discussed privately. Sometimes you can "make time" during class while students are doing their individual work, either stepping outside the door or speaking with them quietly at your desk. This works great for prevention, for problem-solving, and for first-time disciplinary situations. You might want to mention at the time that you prefer to spend *class* time helping students with their work, so that if the situation occurs again, you'll need to discuss it with them *after class*. You are thus explaining the boundaries ahead of time so there will be no surprises. For repeat occurrences of a disciplinary situation or for *BIG* incidents, I always preferred to discuss it with the student *after* class, because this, in itself, is a consequence!

What if a student says he *won't* stay, or that "you can't *MAKE* me stay"? To that simply respond in a friendly but concerned way, "We really *do* need to talk privately. I'll be happy to have you back in class as soon as we can find the time to talk. When would be best for you? Would *before* school work better?" If the student responds in a vague or negative way you can add a little pressure in a "nice" way by adding, "I would really prefer to clear this up soon, because if it goes over twenty-four hours, I would need to involve the Assistant Principal or your parent. I would rather keep it between us." Be careful that you do not sound threatening, just concerned, and watch your body language to make sure that you do not appear controlling. You have to be willing to let the student make a bad choice. Then you would need to follow through and contact the Assistant Principal or the parent, as you had indicated.

If you give students a choice, and they refuse to select one, you might want to ask if they can think of a better option. If they come up with something that isn't appropriate, just say, "No, that wouldn't work for me." (If it isn't easily obvious *why* it wouldn't work for you, you can explain why in a matter-of-fact way.) The process works far better with at-risk students if it looks more like adult-to-adult problem-solving with the goal being a win-win solution than if it looks to the student like you are attempting to control him using "choice" as a means to *secure* control. (A

71

statement such as "You can *choose* to do the assignment I've given you either now or during Detention" isn't *really* a choice, and both you and the student know it. If you have already established yourself as a supportive ally and if you regularly give choices within your classes so that your students *don't* feel over-controlled, you can sometimes "get away with" a pseudo-choice such as in this example if you sound a little playful as you say it, and it *would* be far better than a direct order. But too often that is the only sort of choice students get in control-oriented classes, and at-risk students don't buy it!

If you offer a choice and the student refuses either option and won't come up with a reasonable alternative, you can respond, "If you don't want to make the choice, I'm going to have to do it for you. Is that what you want?" Not to choose, *is* to choose! Help the student see that by *not* choosing, he is actually *choosing* that *you* will be the decision-maker!

Sometimes you find yourself having to enforce a rule that neither the student nor you find much sense in, yet it *is* school policy. With situations like these, I have found that the best solution is a combination of EMPATHY and ASSERTION. (Actually this is the best approach even when you *believe* in a rule which the student doesn't agree with.) Start by "active listening" the student's position, to show empathy. ("I know you believe that you learn better with headphones on.") You don't have to *agree* with the student's point of view in order to acknowledge her feelings. By starting with the *student's* position, instead of your own, you are making it far more likely that the student will cooperate. Next, repeat the rule or school policy that you are expected to enforce. ("The principal has told me that I am not to allow anyone to wear headphones during class.") Again use empathy: "So I know you aren't going to like this and I feel bad about it." Then follow with assertion: "But I really can't let you continue to wear them."

At this point it is effective to give a choice: "Would you rather put them in your backpack or have me hold them for you until after class? I can lock them in my desk." If the student asks why she can't just turn them off and keep them around her neck, a good response would be: "But it might be too tempting to have them so close to your ears. I'll get busy and you might start thinking I won't notice. And if you *did* slip them back on, then I'd have to suspend you for 'Defiance of Authority' and I wouldn't want that to happen." You would be making it very clear what would happen with a repeat offense and yet you are doing so in a helpful, not a threatening way. If the student insists on keeping the headphones around her neck, you could say, "Okay, as long as you realize what will have to happen if you put them back on." You would have avoided a confrontation and secured compliance. If the student *does* slip them back on, you can be very sad as you tell her of the impending suspension that you had really tried to avoid!

This approach of involving the student in the solution of the problem is *much* more effective with at-risk students than telling them what they *must* do and then punishing them for resisting, a response which is totally predictable. So much of the effectiveness of this is related to the attitude you project. I once read an old Norwegian proverb which contains a very appropriate message: "In every woman there is a Queen; Speak to the Queen and the Queen will answer!" I have added a verse: "In every woman there is also a witch; speak to the witch and you won't get the Queen!" (Of course the same concept applies to your male students as well!)

Just as it is effective to problem-solve with an individual student to solve a problem, a good strategy for dealing with CLASS PROBLEMS is to involve the entire class in solving the problem. Simply state what you see as the problem, encourage discussion, brainstorm solutions, look at possible consequences, and have the class decide, of course with your guidance and feedback throughout the process. I received a letter from a participant in one of my workshops who was very happy with this approach:

"A big change has taken place with my students, 90% of whom are at-risk. I expressed that I was not happy with the fact that most of them wandered in 5 or 10 minutes late every day and never had pencils. I asked them what we could do about it. They came up with a plan that would get them to class on time with materials ready to go. I would attach points to getting to class on time and for having their pencil. Then on Friday they could spend the points on cokes and candy which I would supply. (The school has a rule about no cokes and candy in class, so this made it all the sweeter!) I agreed to try this system, thinking, "Yeah, right, so this is going to help?" I wish I had a video camera to record what happens every day. Just picture 8 or 10 male probationers, most of whom are over 200 pounds, fighting each other to get in the door before the tardy bell rings, sitting down, and holding a pencil up ready to go. The first day it happened, I had to go into my office and laugh for five minutes. By the way pencils are disappearing fast from other teachers' rooms!"

She want on to say: "I am amazed every day with the things these kids come up with. I am so glad that I have learned (and am still learning) that *I* don't have to have all the answers. These kids come up with great ideas and the best part is that when *they* come up with something, they do it!"

Will she have to bribe them forever? No--eventually she will be able to say, "You're *BEYOND* that" and raise her expectations for them. (They *aren't* going to say, "We're *not* beyond that!")

Class discussions with at-risk students work best when they are short and to the point. If you're upset, wait until you're calm and can talk about how upset you *were* feeling about something--so that it is *past* tense and you can be solution-oriented: "What can we *do* about this?" If the teacher in the above example had seemed angry, she would have gotten very different results.

As I mentioned earlier, it is really important that you *not* get angry or frustrated and allow students to "push your buttons," because that is when you will start reacting in ways which predictably will escalate the situation. Let me emphasize two TRUTHS:

- The *MORE* you try to GAIN CONTROL,
  the *LESS* CONTROL you have!
- The person with the *MOST FLEXIBILITY*
  has the *MOST CONTROL!*

Whenever you approach an at-risk student with the point of view "My way or the highway!", you are going to lose. These students *cannot* let you win, and *you* have more to lose, because you have to monitor your behavior since you want to keep your job! They don't *care* if they get kicked out of school. They *do care* about appearing invincible around their friends So you need to learn, if you haven't already, how to

SIDESTEP YOUR WAY OUT OF A POWER STRUGGLE!

Unconventional approaches work best. You have to be creative and unpredictable. You can't just tell them what to do and expect them to do it simply *BECAUSE YOU SAID SO!* And remember this: If someone tosses you a rope, they can't win a tug of war if you don't pick up the rope!

Humor works especially well. SP's *really* appreciate humor. They feel as strongly about humor as SJ's feel about responsibility! They are forever suggesting that teachers "lighten up." Part of humor is responding in a way which is very different from what the student expects. I love the story about the substitute teacher who took over an "impossible" class of middle school students. At 9 a.m. on the dot, all the students picked up all the books they had and dropped them on the floor! What did the substitute teacher do? She picked up her books and dropped them on the floor and said, "Sorry I was late!" After the class got over its shock, she expressed great admiration for whoever the mystery class organizer was, saying, "Do you *know how hard* it is to organize students your age? I need to know how you did it! Somebody is awesome! Who *are* you? I need your help!" She won them over immediately, and she had few real problems with them from that point on.

Another teacher told me about her experience the first day she began to teach at a prison. She was following the guard to her classroom, when she suddenly became aware that she was surrounded by very large prisoners who began to crowd her. The guard had disappeared, and one extra large prisoner stepped in front of a button on the wall. (She called it a Panic Button!) He asked, "What would you do if we took you down? You wouldn't be able to call for help?" She looked around at the group of them and replied simply, "I guess I would have to flunk you!" Again, she hadn't acted predictably, and her humor and apparent lack of fear were appreciated. A soft, playful approach works *much better* with this population than a hard, demanding one. The teacher said that from that point on, she was accepted and had few problems with them.

Two other creative responses involve alternative middle school students. One boy threatened the teacher with "I'm going to get my Dad. He'll beat you up!" The teacher responded calmly, "I've been *trying* to get in touch with your father...." Another boy had lost control and was reported to be on the school roof shouting obscenities. The teacher asked him to please come down from the roof, to which the student responded with "F___ you, teacher!" The teacher quickly responded in a calm and logical manner, "If you're going to do that, you're going to have to first come down from the roof!" After the student got off the roof, the teacher remained calm, put his arm around the boy's shoulder, commented on how upset he seemed, and asked what he could do to help. The boy calmed down.

One of my teachers had been transferred to us from the mainstream high school. He had had over twenty years of experience attempting to control students, and he had some real problems philosophically trying to fit into our system. I realized that he had made it when he came to tell me of an incident with a student and how he had handled it. The student, we'll call him William, had "kind of" threatened him. In other words, the "words" definitely sounded threatening, but the student was smiling, and all the "witnesses"--other students--liked William better than they liked the teacher! What William had said to the teacher was, "What would you do if I slapped you?" The teacher immediately started walking away from William saying, as he paced, "You know William, I may be fifty years old but I ride my bike fifty miles three times a week, and you smoke. You'd never be able to catch me! Do you know what smoking does to your lungs?" And he proceeded to launch into an impromptu lecture on the dangers of smoking and the value of aerobic exercise. William just stood there, probably thinking, "What about me?" The bell finally rang, and the teacher called William aside and said, "I didn't feel really comfortable about what you said in class today. I made light of it because I wasn't sure, but I'd like to think that we don't have a problem that we need to discuss with the Principal. What do you think? Do we have a problem?" And William answered, "No, I was kidding," to which the teacher responded, "I'm glad, because I really didn't appreciate it and I trust it won't happen again. I'd have to handle it differently if it did." And William never bothered him again.

Many teachers have a hard time thinking of a response on the spot. Instead they tend to think of the perfect thing to say on drive home! I have two suggestions. First, think of typical problems and come up with several possible responses you could use with each one. Review them periodically so they will be fresh in your mind. Then, when a student misbehaves you will be "ready"! Besides, you will feel happy that you have an opportunity to use your creative response, so this cancels out some of the frustration usually caused by student misbehavior. If you honestly can't think of what to say you can always start pacing back and forth while looking at the class, and then say, "I bet you all are wondering what I am going to do about this. I don't know. But I bet I'll have it figured out by the time class is over. Maria, I'll see you after class." Then you can proceed with the lesson. (Mendler, 1992).

If Maria says, I'm *not* staying after class, you can say to her (privately and in a supportive way), "I'll be happy to have you back in class as soon as we've been able to have our talk. Perhaps *before* school would be better. You let me know. But it has to be within twenty-four hours to keep it just between us, without having to involve the Assistant Principal and a parent. I hope we can solve it without it going that far. By the way, if you change your mind about the after-class meeting, I'll be here until (name a time). And I get here at (name a time) in the morning. It's up to you." You are putting the student in charge and setting the conditions so that the student will know it is to her benefit to meet with you within the time frame you have set to keep the situation from becoming a bigger one, undoubtedly with bigger consequences.

I can't overstate the effectiveness of using active listening when students seem upset. Even if you think what they are upset about is stupid, you're telling them so will *not* solve the problem; it will simply add on additional stress. Just feeling *heard* is often enough to help the student calm down, whereas trying to talk the student out of a feeling tends to escalate it. If you say "I bet you were *really angry* when he said that!", he will feel understood and you can begin to talk with him about how he wants to handle the situation. If instead you say something like "You shouldn't feel that way; he was probably only kidding", the student will need to further convince you that he is right in feeling the way he does, thus "locking in" his attitude. Here are some "stock" responses that you can use, even when a student is upset with you or with the class:

- "I can see that you feel very strongly about this..."
- "I can see why you'd be upset..."
- "I never looked at it that way before..."
- "I'm going to have to think about it. Let's talk later."

You can also ask questions, if it seems appropriate, in an attempt to clarify either the student's thinking or your own understanding:

- "What makes you think that?"
- "What do you think should be done?"
- "I'm not sure I understand. Could you tell me more?"

If the student is handling his frustration or anger by saying something inappropriate, you can use *both* empathy and assertion:

- "I can see you're really angry, but we don't speak to each other that way in this class. I'll be happy to listen to you further when you can speak in a more respectful way."

I love the story of how a teacher handled a student who had blown up and called the teacher a f____ing (w)itch. The student seemed so out-of-control that the teacher felt that nothing she could say could defuse the situation. So she picked up a tablet and started to write. The student became very curious and demanded to know *what* she had written, as he was very sure it was about him. She responded that it was about how sad she was that he was acting this way because she had always liked him and felt that they had a good relationship, and that this was "not *like* him." He asked to read it. He calmed right down and then asked: "What do you mean 'It's not like me'?" What followed was a positive discussion between them.

Another example involved a student who was upset in class and refused to sit down. The teacher responded quietly and empathetically, "You seem *really* upset. Why don't you sit down and tell me about it?" The student sat down. How different the student's response would have been if the teacher had interpreted this as an act of defiance and as a disciplinary incident! Gentler is better!

If you have to deny a request about something the student feels strongly about, you can soften the reaction through empathy:

- "I know you're going to be disappointed, but the answer is going to have to be no this time. I'm sorry.... but I *know* you can handle it."

Such empathetic responses are used heavily by counselors and are easy to use in a one-to-one interaction. When the entire class is listening, it can become more complicated. This is why some interactions need to be saved, if possible, for times when the other students are doing individual assignments or for after class, at your discretion. But student crises often come at inopportune times, perhaps right in the middle of a group lesson. You don't know what the problem is and you don't have time to talk right then. You just know the student is acting in a way that seems inappropriate. You will get a much better response if you don't handle the situation in a disciplinary way. The student is already stressed. To achieve a de-escalation instead of the further escalation of a negative attitude, appear concerned instead of angry. Here are the steps that make up

"THE PROCESS."

→ Defuse yourself.

→ Use active listening to defuse the student.

→ Use "I-Messages" to defuse yourself.

→ Give Choices.

→ Aim for a Win-Win Solution.

Let's say that a student comes into class late, obviously really upset, and slams her books down on the desk, and then mutters an obscenity in response to something another student whispers to her. You could go up to her with a concerned look and quietly say: "You seem *really* upset. I wish I had time to talk to you right now but I don't. I can talk in fifteen minutes or so, after we're done with this experiment. Can you wait, or do you need to talk to someone now?" And then honor the student's choice. That type of interaction is often enough to calm the student down. If she responds that she can wait to talk to you--great! If she responds that she needs to talk to someone else right now--also great! Meanwhile you can attend to your class.

Sometimes a "time-out" is needed. But this has to be seen as the *student's* choice--as an *opportunity* for him to pull himself together without penalty--and not as *your* attempt to control, especially when the student is already stressed and "on the edge"! To mandate a time-out at such a time will almost certainly result in an escalation of the situation and a locking in of positions.

A time-out room, staffed by a "counselor-type" is probably the best solution for a school. However, not all schools can afford this. You might want to arrange, with another teacher, to temporarily "trade" students needing timeouts. A change of classrooms is often enough to break a pattern of student behavior, and such an arrangement will give you a break. You in turn can return the favor.

Some teachers routinely refer misbehaving students to the Office. Whether this is a good strategy depends, of course, upon *who* is in the Office! But even the best administrators and counselors are often in a conference or meeting or otherwise occupied; besides, they wouldn't have the benefit of knowing what happened other than through the student's eyes. As a result, these sessions are not always productive. The student returns to your class with more-or-less the same attitude, at least toward you, that he or she had before.

If you *do* want someone else to intervene. I believe that it is far more effective to schedule a meeting at a non-crisis time so that you can talk with the intermediary beforehand. Then you won't have to spend the session "telling" on the student, because the third party will already know your point of view and can more effectively work toward a solution. You will then be able to show empathy toward the student and during the three-way conversation share some strengths you have seen. It will be much more likely that you and the student will come to some sort of agreement this way.

When all else fails with a difficult student, you might want to try the **paradoxical method**. This involves your reassuming control with an oppositional student by telling the student to do what you know he is going to do anyway, but usually with the situation changed slightly so that the behavior no longer looks as appealing. This approach puts you back in charge *without* engaging in a power struggle, and it makes the student's choice of a negative behavior less desirable. It might even result in the student arguing *your* position. See page 83 for five examples of this approach.

It is also important to anticipate potential problems *before* they

THE PARADOXICAL APPROACH

When a student refuses to do what you ask and you can see no other solution, the Paradoxical Approach can help you regain control without it looking that way. Simply tell the student to do what he/she is doing anyway, but with slightly changed conditions so that the behavior no longer looks as appealing. Then whether the student chooses to follow your original request or your revised one, he/she is following your instructions! For this approach to work, you must make sure to be polite and matter-of-fact, and not sound like you are *trying* to win a power struggle. This approach is especially effective with the SP, who needs to feel "free" and dislikes being told what to do, and also with any student who has locked into a power struggle. Five examples follow:

(1) A student replies emphatically that he will NOT stay in class after you have asked him to take his seat. You say, "You're right. It's better that you leave. I'll call the Office so they can tell your Mom you need to go home."

(2) A student insists she *has* to go on a job interview, and you believe she is just making this up. You say she *should* go to the interview and add that all you need is either her mother's or the potential employer's phone number so you can call to get the clearance that is needed by the Office.

(3) A student is refusing to go to his Science class, saying that it's "boring." You suggest that he drop it since he doesn't like it. He replies that he can't graduate without it. You mention that not everyone graduates and besides, maybe he can take it in Summer School.

(4) All of your students keep talking in class in spite of your repeated requests that they quiet down. You tell them that communication seems to be the major issue of the moment and that you would like them all to talk for the next two minutes to get it out of their systems. Then you ceremoniously set a timer for two minutes.

(5) You tell a student who is chronically disobedient: "I'm getting help learning how to give consequences to students who aren't following the rules. Could you please help me out by disobeying me several times this week so I can practice?"

© 1995 by Vicki Phillips

occur and to intervene in a way that prevents their occurrence. Think about any changes in the schedule or special activities or remarks you've heard students make--anything which could spell trouble. Then, call any student you are worried about aside, express your concerns, and problem-solve with him or her about how the situation could best be handled--*instead* of waiting for the worst to happen and then punishing the student for breaking the rules!

Remember, the goal here is positive youth development and the teaching of responsible decision-making. Our at-risk students are "works-in-progress." We need to *teach* them how to keep from "hooking in" automatically to other people's behavior, and to remember to think of the possible consequences *before* acting. They do not learn this by being punished. What they learn from punishment is that they dislike school and their teachers as well! Disciplinary situations offer teachers an excellent opportunity to "model" for everyone else how someone can *keep* from hooking in to an attempt to push one's buttons. Any teacher response which *escalates* tension and power struggles is counterproductive to the teaching of pro-social skills.

I especially like this excerpt by Haim Ginott (from his book *TEACHER AND CHILD*, 1976) which seems to capture the essence of this Chapter on **Defusing Problem Behavior** better than anything further which I could say.

HAIM GINOTT'S
FRIGHTENING CONCLUSION

"I have come
to a frightening conclusion:
It is my personal approach
that creates the climate.
It is my daily mood
that makes the weather.
As a teacher,
I possess tremendous power
to make a child's life
miserable or joyous.

I can be a tool of torture
or an instrument of inspiration.
I can humiliate or humor, hurt or heal.
In all situations, it is *my response* that
decides whether a crisis will be
escalated or de-escalated,
and a child
humanized or de-humanized."

--Haim Ginott,
TEACHER AND CHILD

DEBRIEFING
DISCIPLINE PROBLEMS

The *real* learning takes place during the Debriefing Stage, during which you and the student discuss the situation as well as what is to happen now. To be effective, this conversation must be private, so that you can gain the student's undivided attention. The approach should be collaborative, with a problem-solving focus: **"You and I against the problem."** The goal is four-fold:

- to help the student see the situation in a *different* way;
- to get the student to "own" the problem so that he or she can *learn* from it;
- to decide what needs to be done to "fix" the problem;
- to help the student develop a sense of em**po**we**r**ment and *self*-discipline.

For this type of session to be effective, the eventual consequences have to be uncertain at this point. This uncertainty as to what might happen is what gets the student's attention and causes her to be interested in discussing the situation with you. She has hopes of influencing the outcome. This is why I don't like automatic, predictable penalties; the student *knows* she is going to get a three-day suspension so what is the use of talking to you? She might as well leave and begin her three-day vacation!

The *least* effective approach at this stage is to lecture the student. Students have heard it all before and it simply doesn't "take!" If you want a student to listen, you have to start from where *he* is, not from where *you* are. Plan to do more listening than talking, with most of the talking that you *actually* do being a balance of asking questions and *active*-listening, where you are paraphrasing what the student has said to show understanding. Research shows that students who do more talking in such sessions *make more positive changes* than those who do more listening. At-risk students don't want to be told what to think any more than they want to be told what to do. So whatever you *tell* them gets blocked. But by listening, you are helping them become less defensive, and by asking questions, you are indirectly guiding their thinking, and they *do* listen to themselves! (You simply need to get them to say the right things by asking the right questions!)

A good approach is to start by commenting on the behavior, non-judgmentally, from how the *student* probably sees it.

- For talking in class too much, you can start by saying something like "Communicating with your friends seems very important to you."
- For cracking too many jokes in class you can start with something like "It sure seemed like you wanted to pump some humor into my class today."
- For causing an outburst in class, "It seemed to me that you felt strongly about something and you really wanted to be heard."

By your starting the conversation this way, the student will feel more understood. Then he will be more likely to listen to *your* concerns, as long as you express them in a problem-solving, not a blaming, way, and use "I-Messages."

I really like William Glasser's Reality Therapy model of asking "What" and "How" questions. Given the way an acting out student *sees* the situation, his behavior fits perfectly; otherwise he would have *acted* differently. What you need to do is to get him to *see* the situation in a different way, so that *he* will decide that his behavior was inappropriate. "What" and "How" questions, coupled with your interest and concern, not blame, can effectively help accomplish this. Questions should be asked in a caring, interested way (which do not "feel" like interrogation) and which are followed each time by active listening.

A list of generic questions follows, although the questions can be personalized to fit any situation. (Notice that there are no "Why" questions. You don't want to ask a student "Why" did he or she do something because then you will simply be given an *excuse!*)

- What happened?
- What were you trying to make happen?
- How would that have helped you?
- What actually happened?
- What will happen now?
- How do you feel about that?
- What do you think will happen if you *keep* doing that?
- Can you think of a different way you could have accomplished it (your goal) without the negative consequences?
- How could you have handled it better in a different way?
- What is your plan now?
- How can I help?

According to Glasser, all behavior is purposeful. Your goal during Debriefing should be to help the student pragmatically *evaluate* the behavior which created the problem. What worked? What didn't work? What *consequences* occurred as the result of the choices made? What problems has he caused for himself? What could he do differently next time? How can he "fix" things now?

In the process, you will have to help the student "reframe" many of his concepts of what power, control, and responsibility actually are. You will guide him, through your questions, to see the relationship between his choices and the consequences he "earned," and to look at the situation from other points of view. Through your questions you will be modeling a more effective decision-making process, one which he will hopefully learn to use in time without your assistance. Your goal should be to help the student accept responsibility for his own behavior. Your questions should be directed toward what the student chose to *DO* rather than his opinions about what happened TO him because of others. (This fits in with the philosophy of empowerment taught in *PERSONAL DEVELOPMENT.)*

If a student is angry and won't talk at first, you can start the process by "walking her through her thinking process" by active listening what she seems to be projecting through her body language. (e.g.-- "You seem to be feeling very angry. I bet you thought he would react differently to what you said, and so now you don't know *what* to think....It hurts to be treated poorly by someone you thought was a friend.") If you are guessing it right and seem concerned and understanding, the student will probably open up. If you are wrong, she will probably let you know you're off-base and then explain what *really* happened.

For disciplinary incidences, there *must* be consequences for chronic offenders if problem-solving is to be effective. Otherwise the student will just think she "got-over" on you by telling you her sad story. This is not what you want. At-risk students usually respect action more than words. Consequences can help students *learn* from their experiences--but *only* if they are handled correctly. If you handle Debriefing in an angry way, a student won't be able to see the connection between the consequence and the choice she made. She will be distracted by your attitude and won't be able to get past the fact that she is angry at you! Too often the opportunity to learn is destroyed by the teacher's or administrator's attitude.

Remember, It takes a *positive* attitude to overcome a *negative one*. And, it is much more effective to give consequences with *empathy* than with anger!

What can you do if a student, in an attempt to avoid consequences, tells you a story which you don't believe is true? It can be quite effective to ask yet another question: "What is more important to you--getting out of the consequences or having me continue to trust your word?" Of course, this will work only if you have built a good relationship with the student; if you haven't, he might not care *what* you think!

Sometimes the consequences happen without your having to give them (e.g.--a student being told he can't take the bus to school because of his poor bus behavior, or not being allowed to eat in the cafeteria for a month because of negative behavior there). Other times consequences can be the attitudes of the other students. You can help the student come up with a *plan* to fix the problem perhaps by making amends in some way. Brainstorm possibilities with the student. Make creative suggestions. Students who are involved in designing the solution are much more likely to carry it through and to learn from the overall experience. This opportunity is lost whenever there is a rigid list of predetermined penalties.

Some educators get trapped by the "fairness" issue. Don't we need to always give the same penalty for the same infraction to be fair? Having penalties be the same for all students *isn't* always fair. Call one student's parents and he might get grounded for a month. Call another student's parents and they might laugh, remembering that they used to do the same thing when they were her age!

Fritz Redl once said the following: "What counts most in punishment is *not* what we do *to the kid* but what the kid *does with* the experience afterwards." When a student is suspended from school for five days after being given a stern lecture during which he rolls his eyes and doesn't listen, do you think he will stay home and think about how he needs to shape up?" Absolutely not! Receiving consequences alone is *not* enough to promote change. It is the positive interaction about the incident with a caring adult which best promotes change. This is why *how* you debrief is so critical!

For chronic problems, I sometimes liked to use a paradoxical negotiating approach. You can say: "I have to give you a BIG enough consequence to 'get your attention' or you'll keep doing this!" Then you can let the student try to *convince* you that it won't take that much. He will undoubtedly suggest a lighter penalty. Suggest he put this in writing on a contract form. You can have his suggestion be the penalty *this* time (or negotiate a stronger version if his is too "soft"), but your very strong penalty will occur if there *is* a next time.

Negotiating and deal-making are effective strategies. Let the student "plea bargain." By handling a chronic problem this way you are, in effect, creating enough of a crisis for the student to motivate him to come up with his *own* strategy to solve it. (Be careful to drive a hard bargain, however, because many of these students are very good negotiators!) When a student manages to come up with his own solution and actually follows through, he develops a sense of efficacy or personal power. You can then reinforce him, *not* for being "good," (which at-risk students don't necessarily aspire to!) but for being *powerful* enough to be able to follow through on a personal commitment! Tell him how *impressed* you are, and that you are sure he is very proud of himself! On the other hand, if he *doesn't* live up to the terms of his contract, you can be sad about the fact that *your* consequence must automatically go into effect.

It is extemely important, as you handle debriefing, that you keep your expectations of the student positive. Students tend to rise either up to, or down to, our expectations. A good phrase to memorize and

STEPS IN NEGOTIATING FOR BEHAVIOR CHANGE

- Set yourself up as an ally of the student.

- Problem-solve with the student about behavior which is interfering with his success. Be matter-of-fact and non-blaming.

- Suggest your opinion about the *best* solution (for a student's problem behavior), making sure it is something that the student absolutely *wouldn't want* (like dropping a class and taking it in summer school!).

- Let the student try to talk you out of your solution and come up with his own "better" solution. Allow him to attempt to convince you that he can do what you actually want him to do. Be a little reluctant.

- Suggest that the student put his suggestion in contract form in his own writing, with your suggestion serving as the backup consequence. (Make sure that this backup consequence is BIG ENOUGH to motivate him to follow through.)

- Be surprised and impressed when the student follows through. If he doesn't, be sad that your consequences must automatically go into effect.

© 1997 by Vicki Phillips

to use on a regular basis during disciplinary conferences is "That wasn't *LIKE* you!" The student might ask, in surprise, "What do you mean?", which gives you the chance to review his or her assets!

Through the debriefing conference, you should attempt to move students from the position of VICTIM, where they are defensive and reactive and blaming others, to a *POWERFUL* position where they begin to "take charge of" their lives and see the choices they *do* have. When they make a mistake, this is an opportunity to underline the truth that failure is never final, and to help them *learn* from the incident and plan how they will deal with similar situations in the future. Since students act the way they *see* themselves, a good debriefing session ends with the student's picture of himself or herself changed for the *better,* not for the worse. I always felt I had done a good job when the student would thank me on her way out the door after I had had to suspend her!

Learn to *welcome* discipline problems as "teachable moments"! Don't look at such times as a distraction from your mission of teaching curriculum. The most important thing you can do for at-risk students is to build a *positive* relationship with them and then help them change any *negative* attitudes. Crises present golden opportunities to build attachments and to teach new, improved attitudes. I would much rather have a student "act out" in school and be able to work with him and help teach him better ways to handle his stress or anger than to read in the newspaper in a few years that he had "gone off" with a semi-automatic weapon in a post office or a MacDonalds'. I have sometimes wondered how many people in prison for murder were ever in a fight in school. I imagine that many of them were--and I assume they were sent home on a five-day suspension to "teach them that they are to follow the rule forbidding fights on campus." Even *if* the suspension did that much, which I doubt, it obviously did not teach them how to handle their emotions or access *self*-control.

The recent rash of school shootings has taught us that we cannot protect our school environments through a Zero Tolerance policy alone. It is not enough to have a school policy and a set of procedures around the issue of eliminating troubled students and then simply turn them out into the community without assistance.

Most discipline plans *disempower* students. The emphasis is on what they *can't* do. As we have discussed time and again, when you try to control at-risk SP students, you in-effect lock them into the very behavior you want changed--and the behavior *escalates*! Their misbehavior is often a symptom that they feel *over*-controlled. In contrast, by attempting to *empower* students, you end up having more, not less, control! This seems paradoxical, but it is more often the paradoxical which works in dealing with these students!

Educators are always talking about the concept of RESPONSIBILITY. I believe that with the Traditional Discipline model, educators are not assuming *their* responsibility of attempting to prevent student problems--or of teaching students the skills they need to be able to handle their problems. The traditional disciplinary model requires that students meet the staff where the *staff* is. In contrast, Empowering Discipline requires that the staff *assume responsibi-lity* for meeting the students where *the students* are and then for helping move them in the right direction.

Schools are the only institution in society which requires, by law, that students be in attendance five or six hours per day nine months of the year for twelve or thirteen years. We can use this power to either further frustrate frustrated students--or to help them. Many students seem to be standing at the edge of a steep cliff. We have a choice. We can either offer our hand and gently assist them back from the edge, or we can push them over. We need to stop seeing student misbehavior as a distraction from the *real* mission of school, which is to teach curriculum. Everything starts looking different when you start seeing your *real* mission as being the positive development of your students. Curriculum is a *part* of this.

You can look at student misbehavior in yet another way--as a golden opportunity to develop and practice the skills which will make you a great teacher! Some students are easy--anyone could be their teacher. This is not the case with at-risk youth. They require great patience and creativity. Your response in any situation may be critical to the what the student's response will in turn be. Of course you'll make some mistakes along the way, but, thanks to the at-risk students, you will have more and more opportunities to practice! Some of the best teachers I know are those who work with the most difficult kids. So from now on, every time a student acts up, tell yourself: "Here's one more opportunity for me to develop my *GREATNESS* as a teacher!"

I am sure there are many of you who face a number of constraints within your Districts--policies and procedures--which will keep you from implementing some of the suggestions within this book. But there is one thing that no District can control, (unless you *let* them) and that is your ATTITUDE! And your attitude is the most powerful tool you have for changing student behavior!

When students express *their* frustration, don't hook in. *Decode* their attitude. They are probably frustrated over the same policies which sometimes frustrate you. Don't take it personally. If it seems to be directed toward you, remember that you represent the educational system to your students. But EMPATHY can tear down the wall which students so often build to protect themselves. Once you are on the same side of the wall as your students, you can be very effective in helping "turn them around". You can help them form new pictures of who they *really* are, knowing that *this* is what must happen *before* their behavior can change!

CONCLUDING THOUGHTS

For years educators have accepted without question the Control Paradigm. Yet many teachers have quietly questioned some of its assumptions, especially NF's (who make up 35% of high school teachers and an even greater percentage of elementary school teachers) and also those SJ's and SP's who prefer to use a "feeling" approach rather than an analytical one when it comes to working with students. Some NT's, who aren't keen on "control" anyway, question this model as well.

The classroom behavior of many of these teachers often reflects the assumptions of Empowering Discipline more closely than it does the Traditional Model. But there has been no theory of discipline they could turn to and quote from when their actions are questioned by those "in charge." They find themselves regularly asking for "leniency" or a "second chance" for students with whom they have been working closely, only to be told that they are being naive and unrealistic, and that "a rule is a rule and we can't make exceptions for individual students, because that would be undermining the system." The teacher is seen as being "soft" instead of as an advocate for a different approach toward discipline, but one which shares the same goal--the improvement of student behavior.

Such growth-promoting teachers are very popular with their at-risk students, who see them as persons they can trust. These teachers discover and draw out strengths from these students that no one, not even the students themselves, knew they possessed.

When these teachers attempt to involve troubled students in creative problem-solving to look for a win-win solution, they often find themselves frustrated with the long list of school procedures, rules and automatic penalties which keep their hands pretty much tied. They sometimes find themselves not sharing information with the administration for fear of the automatic impact it could have on students with whom they are closely working. They realize that anyone can make a mistake, and when there *is* a crisis, they look at the *WHOLE BIG PICTURE* through the lens of positive youth development and see the crisis in perspective.

Such teachers make marvelous breakthroughs daily with students the system has given up on. Yet they constantly face the fear that a favorite student will be suspended or expelled for defiant and disrespectful behavior toward another teacher who is *known* for being disrespectul toward students and for provoking crises. They don't think the "double standard" is fair and wish that the same standards regarding interpersonal relationships could apply to staff *as well as* students.

I have written **EMPOWERING DISCIPLINE** with such teachers in mind. Please carefully review page 99 and compare the **EMPOWERING DISCIPLINE** versus TRADITIONAL DISCIPLINE paradigms item by item. You now have a philosophy to turn to when you confront the "system" to help a student! By sharing your rationale, you will probably make "converts", because many teachers would be open to an different view if they *knew* of one!

To those of you who are open to "conversion", please try the strategies I have suggested in this book. You will discover that *THEY WORK!* The less you worry about controlling your students, the *more* control you will find that you *do* have! Why? Because the students no longer *need* to resist you! Of course, this paradigm switch involves more than simply dropping the Control Issue. In its place you need to substitute "Choice" and the other strategies designed to put the students "in charge"! Meanwhile you can enjoy your new job as **Ally, Encourager, and Supporter,** in order to give your students the *Hope* that they must have before they can develop the *Responsibility* they need. In your spare time you will become a **Systems Organizer.** (Your task, remember, is to control the *system*, not the *students*!) Then, when problems arise, you become the **Defuser,** and later on, the **Debriefer** and *Co-* **Problem-Solver.** *(Your partner in Problem-Solving is always the student involved.)* You will find that this new job description is a lot less stressful and more fulfilling than your current one, and you will feel more successful at it than you do right now!

To remind you of the students you will be helping, I have included the inspiring "Circle of Courage" poem on page 100. If we each "redraw our circles" to include the many students whom schools are failing to reach, together we will make a major impact upon youth and upon society. We simply have to change our paradigm! You can start the process in your own classroom and then advocate for others to do the same. You will find that you will enjoy the process!

I also offer you, as comic relief, "A Horse Story," (page 101). I like it because it reminds me that the Educational Establishment needs to adopt my favorite motto:

"If it doesn't work, don't do it!"

Keeping your sense of humor alive helps prevent burn-out--and leads to a longer and more enjoyable life! So keep smiling; it's contagious, and your students will love you for it! **GOOD LUCK!!**

EMPOWERING DISCIPLINE

• Is proactive--Seeks to *prevent* problem behavior

• Focuses on developing student STRENGTHS

• Attempts to *draw out* the student's *positive* side

• Emphasizes that to *get* respect, you must *give* respect

• Encourages the teaching of pro-social skills and attitudes

• Considers the impact of the curriculum & learning styles upon success

• Links *desired* behaviors with *incentives*

• Considers the reaction of the teacher to disciplinary situations as being critical to the outcome

• Emphasizes prevention, intervention, and rehabilitation

• Has a goal of positive youth development & teaching of decision-making

• Emphasizes brainstorming and problem-solving with the student

• Includes asking for student input and using negotiation as a strategy

• Looks for *creative* consequences

• Aims for a win-win solution

• Assumes that positive interaction w/ a caring adult best promotes change

• Sees misbehavior as an opportunity to help students learn from mistakes

• Works with *all* students, even those who resist the traditional approach

TRADITIONAL DISCIPLINE

• Is reactive--Starts with listing the rules and the consequences

• Emphasizes "fixing" student deficiencies and WEAKNESSES

• Attempts to *control* the student's *negative* side

• Demands respect from students at all times but not always from teachers

• Explains clearly all rules and procedures to be followed

• Ignores the impact of the curriculum & learning styles upon behavior

• Links *negative* behavior with *punishment*

• Does not consider the personal reaction of the teacher as a factor when evaluating disciplinary situations

• Emphasizes control (via rules) and punishment (via consequences)

• Has a goal of maintaining the status quo of the institution (Zero Tolerance)

• Tells students what they *must* do (an authority-centered model)

• Sets rigidly predetermined consequences for each violation

• Uses *predictable* consequences

• Aims for obedience and compliance

• Assumes that receiving consequences best promotes change

• Sees misbehavior as a distraction from the school's *real* mission

• Does *not* work with students who "don't want to be told what to do!"

© 1998 by Vicki Phillips

THE CIRCLE OF COURAGE

by Janna and Larry K. Brendtro

They draw a circle to shut us out.
An anxious bravado concealing their doubt.
Though looks full of loneliness beg us to stay,
Our eyes do not meet; we hurry away.

The school draws a circle to shut them out--
Disrespectful, disruptive, disturbed no doubt.
"If you're not here to learn, you need not stay."
This lesson they master; we drive them away.

He drew a circle to shut me out.
Heretic, rebel, a thing to flout.
But love and I had the wit to win.
We drew a circle that took him in.

by Edwin Markam

Circles that close to keep others at bay
Can yet be redrawn to make "we" out of "they."
Then surrounded by friendship, no longer forlorn.
Discouragement ends,
and courage is born.

A HORSE STORY

Common advice from knowledgeable horse trainers includes the adage, "If the horse you're riding dies, get off." Seems simple enough, yet, in the education business we don't always follow that advice. Instead, we choose from an array of other alternatives which include:

1. Buying a stronger whip.
2. Trying a new bit or bridle.
3. Switching the riders.
4. Moving the horse to a new location.
5. Riding the horse for longer periods of time.
6. Saying things like : "This is the way we've always ridden the horse."
7. Appointing a committee to study the horse.
8. Arranging to visit other sites where they ride dead horses more efficiently.
9. Increasing the standards for riding dead horses.
10. Creating a test for measuring our riding ability.
11. Comparing how we're riding now with how we did ten or twenty years ago.
12. Complaining about the state of horses these days.
13. Coming up with new styles of riding.
14. Blaming the horse's parents. The problem is often in the breeding.
15. Tightening the cinch.
16. Continuing to beat the dead horse.

--Author Unknown

THE "OTHER" THREE LEARNING STYLES

NF LEARNING STYLE: (ABSTRACT RANDOM)

NF learners learn best in a people-oriented, personal, and cooperative atmosphere where they feel valued and where their strengths are recognized and appreciated. They like it when the teacher has a sense of humor and works to establish a warm, positive relationship with them and the class. They do well with Cooperative Learning, where there is a lot of positive interaction between students. They NEED to have some time to talk with others and to be able to express themselves and their feelings creatively. NF's feel stressed and emotional if they feel misunderstood, not valued, criticized, or not listened to. NF students like to learn abstract concepts, and don't like to learn facts. Therefore, they prefer essay tests over the objective type. NF's like to be given the opportunity to use their imagination and creativity. They like to have variety in the routine. They don't like to compete, unless it is just for fun because they are cooperative. NF's LEARN TO HELP UNDERSTAND THEMSELVES AND OTHERS.

NT LEARNING STYLE: (ABSTRACT-SEQUENTIAL)

NT students learn best when they are intellectually stimulated by new ideas and concepts--especially abstract ones. They have a strong need to understand "Why" and to see things logically. They want freedom and autonomy in their pursuit of knowledge. They like exploring new ideas, seeking new knowledge, and solving problems. They dislike oversupervision and busywork which they see as demeaning. NT's like to be appreciated for their academic competence, and they need to be challenged. They get stressed by too many rules and a confining academic structure. NT students must be able to respect a teacher's competence, or they can become critical and difficult. They do well with Independent Study. NT's LEARN BECAUSE THEY LOVE TO LEARN.

SJ LEARNING STYLE: (CONCRETE SEQUENTIAL)

SJ's learn best in a well-structured classroom with clearly defined course content, regular routines, step-by-step instructions and clear requirements, rules, regulations. They prefer concrete information presented in a sequential, chronological manner and don't like abstract concepts. They prefer True-False tests with Right-Wrong answers. They do best if they know the "plan" and if given in advance an outline of the material. SJ's have a strong sense of right and wrong and don't often become involved in disciplinary situations. If they do, it is usually because of classroom disorganization, confusion, or irresponsibility of others which frustrates them. SJ's enjoy being placed in leadership roles & like to help others. They do best in traditional school settings. SJ's LEARN BECAUSE THEY'RE SUPPOSED TO!

BIBLIOGRAPHY AND RECOMMENDED READING

Armstrong, Thomas, *MULTIPLE INTELLIGENCES IN THE CLASSROOM*, ASCD, Alexandria, VA, 1994.

Arthur, Richard, *GANGS AND SCHOOLS*, Learning Pub. Inc. 5351 Gulf Dr. Holmes Beach, FL 34281-1338, 1992.

Benard, Bonnie, *FOSTERING RESILIENCY IN KIDS; PROTECTIVE FACTORS IN THE FAMILY, SCHOOL, AND COMMUNITY*, Northwest Regional Laboratory, Portland, Oregon, 1991.

Berens, Linda V., Ernst, Linda K., Robb, Judith E., and Smith, Melissa A., *TEMPERAMENT AND TYPE DYNAMICS--THE FACILITATOR'S GUIDE*, Temperament Research Institute, 16152 Beach Blvd., Suite 179, Huntington Beach, CA 92647.

Bluestein, Jane PhD. *21st CENTURY DISCIPLINE*, I.S.S. Pub., 1925 Juan Tabo NE, Suite B-249, Albuquerque, NM 87112-3359, 1998.

Brendtro, Brokenleg, & Van Bockern, *RECLAIMING YOUTH AT RISK*, N.E.S. Pub., Bloomington, Indiana, 1990.

Brown, Les, *LIVE YOUR DREAMS* (paperback book), Avon Books, New York, 1992.

Bolton, Robert, Ph D., *PEOPLE SKILLS*, a Touchstone Book, Simon and Schuster, New York, 1986.

CONFLICT RESOLUTION, The Community Board Program, Inc., 149 Ninth St., San Francisco, CA 94103, 1987.

THE COPING CURRICULUM, The Rosen Publishing Group, 29 East 21st. St N.Y. 10010.

Curwin, Richard L., *REDISCOVERING HOPE--OUR GREATEST TEACHING STRATEGY*, N.E.S. Pub., Bloomington, Indiana 47402, 1992.

Delunas, Eve, PhD., *SURVIVAL GAMES PERSONALITIES PLAY*, Sunflower Ink Pub., Palo Colorado Rd., Carmel CA 93923, 1992.

103

Divinyi, Joyce, *SUCCESSFUL STRATEGIES FOR WORKING OR LIVING WITH DIFFICULT KIDS,* The Wellness Connection, 125 Highgreen Ridge, Peachtree City, GA 30269, 1997.

Dyer, Dr. Wayne W., *PULLING YOUR OWN STRINGS,* a Funk & Wagnalls Book, Thomas Y. Crowell Pub., N. Y., 1977.

Ellis, Albert and Harper, Robert A., *A NEW GUIDE TO RATIONAL LIVING,* Prentice-Hall, Englewood Cliffs, NJ 1975.

Fairhurst, Alice M. & Fairhurst, Lisa L., *EFFECTIVE TEACHING, EFFECTIVE LEARNING--MAKING THE PERSONALITY CONNECTION IN YOUR CLASSROOM,* Davies-Black, Pub., Palo Alto, CA, 1995.

Fay, Jim & Funk, David, *TEACHING WITH LOVE & LOGIC,* The Love and Logic Press, Inc., Golden. Colo, 1995.

Frankl, Viktor E., *MAN'S SEARCH FOR MEANING,* Washington Square Press, Pocket Books, N.Y., 1984.

Ginott, Haim, *TEACHER AND CHILD,* Avon Books, 1976.

Glasser, William, *CONTROL THEORY,* Harper and Row, NY, 1984.

Glasser, Willilam, *REALITY THERAPY,* Harper and Row, NY, 1965.

Gordon, Dr. Thomas, *TEACHER EFFECTIVENESS TRAINING,* McKay Pub., NY, 1991.

Hamby, John V., *STRAIGHT TALK ABOUT DISCIPLINE,* National Dropout Prevention Center, Pub., Clemson, South Carolina, 1995.

Harmon, Ed and Jarman, Marge, *TAKING CHARGE OF MY LIFE--CHOICES, CHANGES, AND ME,* The Barksdale Foundation, Idyllwild, CA 92349.

Harris, Robert, *I'M OK--YOU'RE OK; A PRACTICAL GUIDE TO TRANS-ACTIONAL ANALYSIS,* Harper & Row, N. Y., 1969.

Hartmann, Thom, *ATTENTION DEFICIT DISORDER: A DIFFERENT PERCEPTION,* Underwood Books, P.O. Box 1607, Grass Valley, CA 95945.

Helmstetter, Shad, *CHOICES,* Pocket Books, N. Y., 1987.

Jamison, Kaleel, *THE NIBBLE THEORY AND THE KERNEL OF POWER,* Paulist Press, N.Y., 1989.

Jeffers, Susan, *FEEL THE FEAR & DO IT ANYWAY,* Ballantine Books, NY, 1987.

Keirsey, David & Bates, Marilyn, *PLEASE UNDERSTAND ME--CHARACTER & TEMPERAMENT TYPES,* Prometheus Nemesis Book Co., Box 2092, Del Mar, CA. 92014, 1978. David Keirsey's Website with the Temperament Sorter Test is http://www.keirsey.com/cgi-bin/keirsey/newkts.cgi

Kohn, Alfie, *BEYOND DISCIPLINE*, ASCD, Alexandria, VA, 1996.

Kroeger, Otto and Thuesen, Janet M., *TYPE TALK*, a Delta Book by Dell Publishing, New York, 1988.

Kroeger, Otto with Janet M. Thuesen, *TYPE TALK AT WORK*, A Dell Trade Paperback, New York, N.Y., 1992.

Kuykendall, Crystal, *FROM RAGE TO HOPE: STRATEGIES FOR RECLAIMING BLACK & HISPANIC STUDENTS*, N.E.S. Pub., Bloomington, IN, 1992.

La Meres, Clare, *THE WINNERS' CIRCLE--YES, I CAN!*, La Meres Lifestyles Unlimited, Newport Beach, CA, 1990.

Lockhart, Alexander, *POSITIVE CHARGES--544 WAYS TO STAY UPBEAT DURING DOWNBEAT TIMES*, Zander Press, P. O. Box 11741, Richmond, VA 23230, 1994.

Maltz, Maxwell, *PSYCHO-CYBERNETICS*, Pocket Books, N.Y, 1960.

Matthews, Andrew, *BEING HAPPY*, Price Stern Loan, Los Angeles, CA, 1988.

McBride, Willian, *ENTERTAINING AN ELEPHANT*, Pearl Street Press, 63 Pearl St., San Francisco, CA 94103, 1997.

McKay, Gary D. & Dinkmeyer, Don, *HOW YOU FEEL IS UP TO YOU--THE POWER OF EMOTIONAL CHOICE*, Impact Pub., San Luis Obispo, CA '94.

McKay, Matthew and Fenning, Patrick, *SELF-ESTEEM*, New Harbinger Pub., Oakland, CA 94607, 1987.

Mendler, Allen N., *HOW TO ACHIEVE DISCIPLINE WITH DIGNITY IN THE CLASSROOM*, N.E.S. Pub., Bloomington, Indiana, 1992.

Minchinton, Jerry, *MAXIMUM SELF-ESTEEM*, Arnford House, Pub., Rt. 1, Box 27, Vanzant, Mo 65768, 1993.

Moawad, Bob, *UNLOCKING YOUR POTENTIAL*, (audio-cassette tape series), Nightingale, Conant Corp., Chicago, Ill.

Myers, Katherine D. and Kirby, Linda K., *INTRODUCTION TO TYPE DYNAMICS AND DEVELOPMENT*, Consulting Psychologist Press, Palo Alto, CA, 1994.

Nelson, Jane & Lott, Lynn, *POSITIVE DISCIPLINE FOR TEENAGERS*, Prima Pub., P.O. Box 1260BK, Rocklin, CA 95667, 1994.

Phillips, Gary, *CLASSROOM RITUALS FOR AT-RISK LEARNERS*, National School Improvement, P. O. Box 1234, Issaquah, WA 98027.

Phillips, Vicki, *PERSONAL DEVELOPMENT*, P. O. Box 203, Carmel Valley, Ca 93924, 1991 (Revised 1996).

Phillips, Vicki, *TURNING THEM AROUND*, P. O. Box 203, Carmel Valley, CA 93924, 1996.

Robbins, Anthony, *AWAKEN THE GIANT WITHIN*, a Fireside Book, Simon & Schuster, N. Y., 1992.

Robbins, Anthony, *NOTES FROM A FRIEND: A QUICK AND SIMPLE GUIDE TO TAKING CHARGE OF YOUR LIFE*, A Fireside Bk, N.Y., 1995.

Schwartz, David, *THE MAGIC OF THINKING BIG*, Simon & Schuster, N.Y.

Seliger Susan, *STOP KILLING YOURSELF--MAKE STRESS WORK FOR YOU*, G. P. Putnam's Sons, N. Y., 1982.

Synowiec, Bertie Ryan, *DOES ANYONE HEAR OUR CRIES FOR HELP? (ACTION STRATEGIES FOR THOSE AT-RISK)*, 28641 Elbamar Dr., Grosse Ile, Michigan 48138

Tieger, Paul D. & Barron-Tieger, Barbara, *DO WHAT YOU ARE (DISCOVER THE PERFECT CAREER FOR YOU THROUGH THE SECRETS OF PERSONALITY TYPE)*, Little, Brown, & Co., N.Y., 1992.

Tobias, Cynthia Ulrich, *EVERY CHILD CAN SUCCEED*, Focus on the Family Pub., Colorado Springs, CO, 1996.

Weiss, Lynn, PhD., *A.D.D AND CREATIVITY*, Taylor Pub., 1550 W. Mockingbird Lane, Dallas, TX 5235, 1997.

Wright, Esther, *LOVING DISCIPLINE--A TO Z*, Teaching from the Heart, P. O. Box 460818, San Francisco, 94146-6818, 1994.

ABOUT
THE AUTHOR

Vicki Phillips was a continuation high school principal for twenty-two years, and a Job Corps counselor and teacher for four years before that. In 1992 her school was selected one of eleven "Model" Continuation High School programs in California, and in 1989 her school won one of five S.T.A.R.S. (Strategies for Teachers of At-Risk Students) awards.

Vicki's main interest has always been changing dysfunctional attitudes and building resiliency in At-Risk adolescents. In 1990 she wrote *PERSONAL DEVELOPMENT*, a one-semester curriculum designed to develop respect, responsibility, and resiliency in at-risk students. In 1996 she wrote a book, *TURNING THEM AROUND: DEVELOPING MOTIVATION, RESPONSIBILITY, AND SELF-DISCIPLINE IN AT-RISK YOUTH*. Vicki's current book, *EMPOWERING DISCIPLINE,* is an attempt to change the paradigm in education to one which will better meet the needs of at-risk youth.

Vicki currently speaks at conferences nationwide about the importance of teaching pro-social attitudes and skills. She also presents one and two-day workshops for individual schools and organizations on Building Responsibility and Self-Discipline, on Personality Temperament and Learning Styles, and on the Teaching of Pro-Social Attitudes and Skills to At-Risk Youth. Over 700 school districts and organizations have purchased *PERSONAL DEVELOPMENT,* as of July, 1998.

Vicki can be reached by mail at P.O. Box 203, Carmel Valley, CA 93924 or by phone: (831) 659-5913 or fax: (831) 659-9109.

OTHER MATERIALS AVAILABLE BY VICKI PHILLIPS

- *PERSONAL DEVELOPMENT Preview Packet*--75 pgs. Includes
  5 sample lessons plus additional information. Send a check, prepaid.
  (No purchase orders or shipping costs for the Preview Packet.) $ 15.00

- *PERSONAL DEVELOPMENT (Group Version)* 530 pgs.* $375.00

- *PERSONAL DEVELOPMENT (Individualized Version)* 452 pgs.* $350.00

- *PERSONAL DEVELOPMENT (Both Group & Individ. Versions)* $595.00
  982 pgs.*

- *TURNING THEM AROUND: Developing Motivation,*
  Responsibility, & Self-Discipline in At-Risk Youth 296 pgs. $ 49.95

- EMPOWERMENT POSTERS--Student Set (40 posters) $ 59.00

- EMPOWERENT POSTERS--Staff Set (40 posters) $ 59.00

- EMPOWERMENT POSTERS--Combined Student & Staff Set $ 99.00

- AUDIO TAPE--60+ minutes--"Building Respect, Responsibility, $ 10.00
  and Resiliency in At-Risk Adolescents"

* The purchase of *PERSONAL DEVELOPMENT* entitles the purchaser to
reproduce any student worksheets or handouts for purchaser's own classes.

** PURCHASE ORDERS: Accepted from schools & other major organizations
on orders of $25 or over. Checks or money orders are required for all other orders.

TAX--CA Residents only: Please add sales tax at your county's rate.

SHIPPING--In U.S., add $15.00 shipping/handling for *PERS.DEVELOPMENT*
                     $ 5.00 for *TURNING THEM AROUND*
                     $ 3.00 for *EMPOWERING DISCIPLINE*
                     $ 3.00 for EMPOWERMENT POSTERS (Single Set)
                     $ 5.00 for EMPOWERMENT POSTERS (Double Set)
                     $ 2.50 for Audio Tape
                     (OVERSEAS AIRMAIL: Add 10% of total)

To place an order or to request more information about any of the above
materials, please write, phone, or fax:

PERSONAL DEVELOPMENT
P.O. Box 203
Carmel Valley, CA 93924

Phone: (831) 659-5913 or (888) 4 AT-RISK
Fax: (831) 659-9109